Hiking Maryland

A Guide for Hikers & Photographers

Scott E. Brown

STACKPOLE
BOOKS

0 11557 00827 2

To my wife Diane
For all that you do and all that you've done.

Copyright ©2014 by Stackpole Books

Published by
STACKPOLE BOOKS
5067 Ritter Road
Mechanicsburg, PA 17055
www.stackpolebooks.com

Printed in USA

10 9 8 7 6 5 4 3 2 1

FIRST EDITION

Design by Beth Oberholtzer
Cover design by Caroline Stover

Cover: Muddy Creek Falls, Swallow Falls State Park
Back cover: Meadow Mountain Tower, New Germany State Park

Library of Congress Cataloging-in-Publication Data

Brown, Scott E., 1962–
    Hiking Maryland : a guide for hikers and photographers / Scott E. Brown.
        pages   cm
    ISBN 978-0-8117-0827-2
    1. Hiking—Maryland—Guidebooks. 2. Photography—Maryland—Guide-
books. 3. Maryland—Guidebooks. I. Title.
GV199.42.M32B3438   2014
796.5109752—dc23
                                                    2013030841

Contents

Introduction

I guess it was around 3:00 A.M. when I finally settled into my sleeping bag after shooting the night sky at Assateague. While skimming the John Muir reader *Journeys in the Wilderness* by headlamp, I came across a quote I must share: "The mountains are calling and I must go."

In all my books, I've worked hard to give you sense of the moment, of what it's like to be on a hike with me or to see and feel what I do, to channel my inner John Muir as it were. To be standing atop the state land highpoint on a crisp fall evening as night descends gives one a profound sense of place. Sitting in an Eastern Shore salt marsh lit by a full moon in the very wee hours of morning is pure magic. Watching an eagle cruise along a river or a nuthatch hop down an ancient tree trunk is mesmerizing. Clinging to some lonely mountain crag during sunrise is a glorious thing. To wander a forest in a spring rain is, well, there's just nothing like it.

Nature doesn't care where you're from or what you do for a living, nor does she worry herself about your physical condition—she merely asks you to venture out and embrace her. Maryland is an incredibly scenic state and you owe it to yourself to explore it in all kinds of weather, during every season, and in every kind of light.

Listen to your inner John Muir: "Maryland is calling, and you must go."

Safety

I would be remiss if I didn't begin by talking about safety with this stern warning: You are solely responsible for your own safety. This guide has a mix of hikes from flat walks along swampland dikes, cliff edges and waterfalls to rugged mountain trails. Although none of them are particularly risky, ledges, cliffs, and waterfalls are inherently hazardous, particularly in winter or by headlamp.

Lightning

Weather is the biggest issue you'll have to deal with, especially the ever-present thunderstorms of summer. Some of the most remarkable photographic light imaginable is found when the weather is changing radically.

Amazing cloud formations tend to precede or follow violent weather. Remember the whole "red sky at night" saying? Seeking spectacular light is what photographers do. The downside to seeking good cloud formations is lightning, and when it comes to lightning don't mess around.

Getting stuck on a mountain or in the middle of marsh during lightning is potentially lethal. The only way to protect yourself is to avoid getting caught. Always check the weather before a hike, and never hike when the forecast has a high probability of thunderstorms. Between May and October, thunderstorms can pop up without warning, especially in the mountains. I use a combination of local radio, weather.com, AccuWeather, and intellicast.com to make my hiking decisions. Even so, I've been caught on ridges in lightning a number of times, and let's just say such occasions provide one a unique focus and motivation to seek safety.

The National Outdoor Leadership School (NOLS) and the National Weather Service Lightning Safety Office have a lot to say about lightning safety. NOLS's John Gookin has written a marvelous article on lightning safety, myths, and science that you can find online. Here are some tips based on his advice:

- Do not put yourself into a position where lightning can become a hazard. In short, do not hike if the forecast is for bad weather.

- If you can see it, flee it. If you can hear it, clear it. If you see lightning or hear thunder, leave the area and seek cover. The best possible cover is an enclosed modern building or other structure. The next best thing is a car, making sure not to touch any metallic surfaces inside the vehicle. Caves of any type are *not* considered good cover.

- Use the 30-30 rule: If the time delay between a lightning flash and the bang is thirty seconds or less, seek shelter immediately. Do not leave shelter until it's been thirty minutes since you heard the last thunder. To calculate the distance to a lightning strike, take the time delay between flash and bang in seconds and divide by 5. A thirty-second delay means a strike is 6 miles away. It's common for thunderstorms to move at 30 miles per hour, so a strike 6 miles away gives you about twelve minutes to seek cover. That's not a lot of time.

- If you are caught in the open and cannot reach a building or vehicle do the following:
  — Quickly get as far off the ridge as quickly as possible, descending as low as you can. Seek a ravine or other depression if possible.
  — Stay away from isolated trees; towers, power lines, or fences; or anything metallic.
  — Drop your equipment and lay down your tripod. Stay a good distance away from both.

Michael Keeler shows how to create the smallest possible target while minimizing contact with the ground. If you get caught by lightning, this is the position of last resort.

— Individuals in groups should disperse as far from each as other as practical; 50 feet of separation is a minimum distance.

— Don't be the tallest thing around. Assume "lightning position," crouching in a tight ball with your feet together, and staying on the balls of your feet.

Cold Weather

Getting into the woods after a snow storm is easier than you might think, and no, you don't need snowshoes, although they do help. Cold weather, in general, and snow, in particular, present a unique set of circumstances that hikers and photographers have to deal with. Cold fingers and chilly feet are the norm for the winter photographer, but hypothermia can set in without your realizing it, so it's important to know the warning signs:

• Shivering that may be controlled with activity is risky, but uncontrolled shivering is serious.

• Hands or feet that become stiff or moving joints that become painful when muscles tense.

• A feeling of fatigue or weakness.

• Skin that looks waxy or pale or feels numb when touched.

If you have any of these warning signs, get out of the cold as quickly as you can. Here's the thing, though: You're not always the best judge of how you feel. It's always a good idea to hike with a buddy in cold weather.

Frostbite is a threat to exposed skin even when it's not windy. Here are some warning signs:

• Skin that becomes white and is hard and cold to the touch.

• Pain or a burning sensation.

• Itching like you have a rash.

• Loss of feeling in the affected area.

• Mottled skin color.

• Skin that becomes red and blotchy when warmed, like a burn.

Even though cold-weather hiking presents some dangers, you can enjoy it by preparing carefully. The key is in understanding how to dress. Here are some things to consider.

- Dress in many layers.
- Use synthetic fabrics designed to move moisture away from the skin. Avoid cotton, which will suck heat away from the body if it becomes wet.
- Wear a good hat and keep your ears covered.
- Wear mittens and thin synthetic glove liners.

The main point to consider is sweating and cooling cycles. While hiking, you'll sweat a lot, but when you stop at a location, you'll quickly get cold. For temperatures around 0°F, here's how I dress. I don a pair of wicking long johns covered by a pair of hiking pants and then rain pants. I use two to three pairs of socks, beginning with a wicking sock followed by pairs of heavy Smart-Wool. I wear leg gaiters and make sure my rain pants are tight around the ankles to keep snow out of my boots. On the upper body, I wear two wicking T-shirts followed by two long-sleeve shirts of increasing thickness. Over this I wear either a fleece vest or jacket topped with a good winter coat or a raincoat as a wind layer. To protect my hands, I use a thin pair of glove liners and high-quality convertible mittens made by Thinsulate. These fingerless gloves have a mitten-like flap that covers the fingers but can be folded back, keeping my hands nice and toasty while allowing me to use my fingers. I wear a good knit hat and a neck gaiter, and I take along one or two bandannas and a pair of earmuffs called 180s.

While hiking, remove layers when you begin to sweat. It's not uncommon for me peel down to my inner layers and wear only a head bandanna at 10°F. Trouble can start when you get to a location and stop moving. Don't wait to cool off before relayering. Immediately put on everything you have, especially a cap. Once you get to a vista, you may not move much again for an hour or more. Good socks and boots mean everything when you're standing still. Never buy inexpensive cold-weather clothing, especially boots. Seek a good outfitter and ask lots of questions.

When it comes to winter fitness, know your limits. You'll exert yourself much more in snow than you anticipate. When there's a foot of snow on the ground, trail difficulties increase—an easy hike becomes difficult and a difficult hike even more so. Unseen rocks will have a thin layer of ice on them, so you're not just walking against greater resistance, you're walking on big slippery marbles as well. Don't fear exploring the winter landscape, just start small.

Winter hiking can also be hard on your camera equipment. Fine, powdery snow blows around easily in the calmest breeze and gets into everything unless care is taken. Here are some pointers:

- Keep your bag closed as much as possible. It doesn't need to be zipped tight; just keep your gear covered.

- Stand up to change lenses, using a coat as a wind break.

- If you drop something in snow, *don't blow on it in order to clean it*. Hot breath will only make matters worse. Use canned air, a squeeze ball, or sable-hair brush to remove snow from equipment.

- Allow your equipment to acclimatize by keeping it in the cold before you shoot. This is easily done by locking it in your car overnight, if you think it's going to be safe.

- When bringing gear in from the cold, put camera bodies and lenses in freezer bags before entering a warm room. This way condensation or frost will form on the bag and not inside an expensive camera. In fact, don't even open the camera bag for a couple hours after coming in, just in case.

- Modern electronic cameras, especially digital equipment, will eat batteries in cold weather. Always carry extra batteries, and keep at least one set in a warm pocket. Make sure there are no coins in that pocket, since powerful batteries can short across loose change and burn you.

Hunting Season

Some of the best times to shoot are also hunting seasons. Almost every hike on state lands is open to hunting. Wooded areas have different issues from marshes. In wooded areas, hunters use all manner of weapons looking for critters on the ground, so wearing orange is an absolute must. In marshes, hunters use shotguns aimed up. I've had the occasional pellet load rain down on me; it's no big deal. Either way, avoid the opening day in any season.

The State Department of Natural Resources recommends everyone, not just hunters, wear blaze orange during all seasons. Here are their rules:

- A cap of solid daylight fluorescent orange color, worn as an outer garment on the head at all times.

- A vest or jacket containing back and front panels of at least 250 square inches of solid fluorescent orange color, worn as an outer garment at all times.

- An outer garment of camouflage fluorescent orange containing at least 50 percent fluorescent orange color worn above the waist.

I recommend putting lots of orange on your pack as well. Do everything you can to be seen easily during dusky lighting conditions. For a list of hunting seasons, check the DNR's website: www.dnr.state.md.us/huntersguide.

Bugs

Needless to say, lots of bugs live in Maryland's many swamps and marshes. This more than anything puts people off, especially ticks. When hiking any Tidewater county, the best way to avoid mosquitoes is to not be around when they are. Any time after the first frost is good, or whenever the temperature is forecast to be low, say around 50°F. A breeze helps, too. If you're stuck with warm-weather travel, use lots of DEET and wear long pants and a light-colored, long-sleeve shirt. I use a head net when no other option exists.

Ticks can be a real problem once the weather gets warm. I've had armies of them marching up my legs, which can be kind of gross. In any Tidewater area, long pants are a must, even if it's hot. Wear light colors, so that you can spot ticks easily. Stick to the center of trails, avoid tall grass, and check yourself often.

If a tick attaches itself to your skin, follow the advice of the Center for Disease Control and Prevention (CDC) and remove it as soon as possible. When hiking, be sure to carry a set of clean, fine-tipped tweezers for this purpose. Grab the tick with the tweezers close to the surface of your skin, pulling up firmly. Avoid jerking or twisting, which may cause the tick's mouth to break off in your skin. Once the tick is removed, clean the bite with rubbing alcohol, iodine scrub, or soap and water. If the tick's mouth does break off on your skin, try to grasp it with the tweezers; however, if the mouth is too difficult to extract, the CDC advises that you clean the bite and let it heal. Contact your doctor if you develop a rash or fever after a tick bite. For more information, see the following post on the CDC website: www.cdc.gov/ticks/removing_a_tick.html.

To put a positive spin on the bug situation, country singer Brad Paisley has perhaps the best sentiment: "I'd like to walk you through a field of wildflowers / And I'd like to check you for ticks." Kind of romantic when you think about it.

Night Hiking

Getting to a sunrise location or returning from a sunset requires hiking in the dark. Night hiking is a unique and, believe it or not, truly fun thing to do. If you've never hiked in the dark, there are some things to take into account beforehand. Perhaps the biggest is how different trails look in the dark and how little you can actually see. By headlamp, your view of the world is only a few feet wide, and at best you can see just a dozen yards ahead. Your color vision isn't reliable, and blazes are difficult to see, landmarks are hard to find and recognize, and drop-offs are almost invisible. Stumbling over rocks is an ever-present problem as well. Simply put, you just can't move as quickly as you can in daylight, so don't try.

Many of the trials in this guide are short in-and-out hikes with few trail intersections. Still, it's easy to walk off a trail in the dark, and finding it again can be difficult. Even when you've moved only a few yards, the trail you were just on can be invisible. Here are some tips on preparing for a night hike:

- Hike the route in daylight as a test.
- Carry a cell phone.

- Carry three forms of illumination. I use a headlamp along with a small flashlight clipped to my pack. I also keep a large flashlight in a pocket. Take along extra batteries for all.

- Move slowly and pause often. Alternate your gaze from your feet to the limit of your headlamp. Trails are easily lost when you only look down at your feet. Pause often, looking to the rear to see if the trail is behind you.

- Carry a good map, compass, and a GPS unit if you have it. Make sure to mark your vehicle position.

- Use trekking poles, which are a help in rocky terrain. If you don't have them, then keep your hands free in case you stumble.

- Stumbling and tripping are inevitable. Learn to fall down gracefully.

- Don't panic. If you lose the trail, take a moment to get your bearings. Then, as carefully as possible, backtrack your route, pausing often and moving just a few yards at a time. If you are completely lost, stay put and *don't panic!* Wait until daylight before attempting to hike out.

Something else to deal with is what can best be described as the willies. Hiking in the dark, especially for the first time, can cause you to imagine all manner of things lurking just out of view. I've often had deer jump in front me, and every time it scares me to death. You just have to get used to it. In darkness animals can see much better than you, and they'll avoid you if possible.

Perhaps the one creature you'll encounter that taps into people's deepest psyche is bats. Bats scare most people more than any animal you can name. Having them zip noiselessly past your head is the admission price for nocturnal hiking, so get used to the idea. Try not to scream, and don't worry—they're after the bugs that your sweat, breath, and headlamp attract. I've found that having bats nearby affords a rare opportunity to observe them at close quarters, and I think they're very cool to have around. Unfortunately, white-nose syndrome has decimated bat populations, so these encounters now occur with less frequency.

Snakes also tend to freak people out. I encountered several rattlesnakes in creating this guide, all of them while hiking across rocks. Their rattling buzz is a unique sound that will get your attention—quickly. It's OK to scream and then jump a few feet out of the way. Typically a snake is only warning you it's there; simply divert several feet around it. Never harm any snake you encounter. Just let it be. The best piece of advice I can give is to never put a hand or foot into any shadow you can't see into. Always use handholds that are well lit.

Ethics and Etiquette

Time and again I've seen amateur photographers come to a location and try to bully their way to a good spot. Some photographers tend to be very intolerant of non-photographers. Respect and common courtesy go a long way toward getting what you want. Words like, "please," "thank you," and "may I," work wonders.

Consider becoming a member of the North American Nature Photography Association. NANPA is a strong proponent of ethical behavior among nature photographers and their ethics principle states as follows:

> Every place, plant, and animal, whether above or below water, is unique, and cumulative impacts occur over time. Therefore one must always exercise good individual judgment. It is NANPA's belief that these principles will encourage all who participate in the enjoyment of nature to do so in a way that best promotes good stewardship of the resource.

To paraphrase some of the NANPA guidelines as they apply to photographing waterfalls, please do the following:

- Stay on trails that are intended to lessen impact.
- When appropriate, inform resource managers or authorities of your presence and purpose.
- Learn the rules and laws of the location. In the absence of management authority, use good judgment.
- Prepare yourself and your equipment for unexpected events.
- Treat others courteously.
- Tactfully inform others if you observe them engaging in inappropriate or harmful behavior. Report inappropriate behavior. Don't argue with those who don't care—report them.
- Be a good role model, both as a photographer and citizen. Don't interfere with the enjoyment of others.

Respect private land. Posted is not a mere notification that the land is privately owned, it is a stern warning to stay off the land. It doesn't matter what you see other people doing; unless you have specific permission to go onto private land, you are in violation of the law and subject to arrest. Respect all private land markers and postings.

DNR land markers will be either yellow signs facing out from the public holding, yellow paint encircling a tree, or yellow paint blobs also facing out. Blue paint of various hues, and sometimes white paint, mark private land boundaries. In cases where DNR or other organizations like The Nature Conservancy (TNC) have access easements there will be signage stating so. There are many who believe that all streams are public land and that if you travel up a creek you're not trespassing. This is a myth. Posted means posted—period.

DNR parking areas for all hunting lands will be signed. If you park along a narrow country road, make sure you're fully off the pavement. Speaking of which, in the Tidewater counties, road edges are deceivingly soft. If you park off the pavement anywhere along the bay when there's no obvious prepared surface, you're in for serious trouble and one big towing bill. Many road surfaces are above the high-tide line by a couple inches, and the road shoulders aren't exactly firm. The contact pressure from a tire will cause the "soil" to flow outward, so while you're watching, your vehicle will slowly sink to the axels. This is what one might call "bad."

How to Use This Guide

Driving distances are provided in miles and road names are given along with the state or county route number, or just the route number when there is no name. The best map to have when using this guide is DeLorme's *Maryland Gazetteer*. The state forest service does not have free public-use maps, so it's a good idea to have a topographic map for those hikes. State park and forest maps cost between $3 and $6, and they're very good; they can be purchased from the various state park visitor centers or online at http://shopdnr.com/trailguides.aspx. National Geographic has a waterproof map set for the Delmarva. The Potomac Appalachian Trail Club has maps for the Appalachian Trail and Rock Creek in Washington, D.C.; these can be purchased from PATC.net. Also, AAA provides metro maps for DC and Baltimore. Finally, a good vehicle GPS is always handy.

GPS coordinates for parking areas and destinations are given in degrees, minutes, seconds format. In many cases the coordinates are from the U.S. Geologic Survey Geospatial Information System database, known as GIS. National Geographic's *TOPO! State* series CD-ROM maps were used to get this information. These GIS coordinates are ground-verified using a Garmin eTREX handheld GPS or Garmin Nüvi 1450. For locations that have no GIS location the eTREX was used to mark the location. Even though a handheld GPS unit might indicate twelve feet positioning accuracy, in reality the number is as much as plus or minus 100 feet depending on the GPS unit's view of the sky. A GPS unit will get you close to a location; finding it is typically done by reading the terrain. Bear this fact in mind where I note GPS coordinates for bushwhacks and trail junctions.

Round-trip hiking distances are in miles. Hiking times are based on a conservative combination of my hike time and Naismith's Rule (allow one hour for every three miles, and add an additional hour for every 2,000 feet of vertical ascent). Hiking times do not include the time needed to set up, compose, shoot, and break down camera equipment. When planning a hike, consider how long you may take to photograph, based on past experience. Always be aware of the clock so as not to be caught unprepared by darkness.

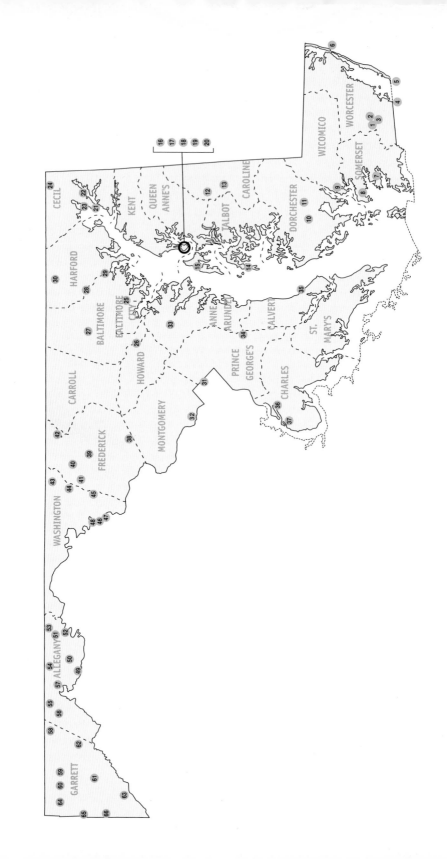

WORCESTER

WICOMICO

SOMERSET

CAROLINE

DORCHESTER

TALBOT

QUEEN
ANNE'S

KENT

CECIL

HARFORD

BALTIMORE

BALTIMORE
CITY

CARROLL

HOWARD

ANNE
ARUNDEL

CALVERT

ST.
MARY'S

PRINCE
GEORGE'S

CHARLES

MONTGOMERY

FREDERICK

WASHINGTON

ALLEGANY

GARRETT

6

5

4

1 2
3

9

7

8

12

13

10

11

24

23 22
21

30

29

28

27

25

26

33

34

35

36

37

31

32

42

39

40

41

43

44

45

46

47

48

38

15

14

51
53

52

54

50

49

57

55

56

58

62

60 59

61

64

63

65 66

16 17 18 19 20

Elevation changes are given in feet from the parking area and are the total elevation gain or loss for the route provided. If you go up 800 feet, then descend 200 feet, the elevation gain will be given as 1,000 feet.

Hikes are rated as easy, moderate, difficult, or strenuous. This is a subjective rating system that combines elevation gain, steepness, and trail conditions into a general statement of what to expect. Hike difficulties are rated on the conservative side. A very fit twenty-five year old may think I'm a sissy for rating a trail as difficult, whereas what I call a moderate hike may be a real bear for someone who's sixty, overweight, and smokes. Take your degree of fitness and experience into account when using these ratings.

The "hand" of stream sides, banks, and edges, such as left-hand and right-hand, is given from the perspective of looking downstream. For example, when I say, "Cross to the left-hand side of the creek at any convenient point," I mean the left side as viewed when looking downstream. Words like opposite, turn, and return are from the perspective of the hiker. For example, when I say, "Turn right and look for an enormous boulder," I mean turn toward your right. In many cases I try to use redundant notations to make sure there's no ambiguity. For example, "From this point turn left (upstream) and walk 2 miles."

Waterfalls and Vista Points

Maryland has a few nice falls, but what exactly is a waterfall? According to the U.S. Geologic Survey there are sixty-three accepted topographic names that could be used to define a waterfall, including fall, ledge, slide, cataract, rapid, riffle, chute, plunge, and drop. As can be seen by this small sample of names, not every fall is a vertical drop from a ledge or overhang as might be expected. Many are tumbles down heavily terraced faces, nearly vertical slides, cataracts, or flume-like chutes. In lieu of a clear USGS definition, the naming criteria for this guide are defined as follows:

Fall: Water plunging from a ledge or precipice that is vertical and/or undercut.

Cascade: A vertical to nearly vertical terraced face where water tumbles down it and is too steep to climb without special climbing gear.

Slide: A near-vertical to less-than-vertical smooth surface, or nearly smooth surface, that is wider than the stream going over it and is too steep to climb without special climbing gear.

Chute: A narrow slide or cataractlike feature that confines the stream flow and is too steep to climb without special climbing gear.

These definitions all have one thing in common: Waterfalls are generally impassable obstructions unless special equipment is used. There are just a few features like this in Maryland and they're all special in their own way. Visit them all.

Maryland's waterfalls are seasonal and so their power and character change quickly from spring's snow melt to summer's heat. Also, their photographability changes from week to week and even day to day because of rainfall. Generally speaking, the best seasons are spring, during the early portion of leaf out, and autumn after a good soaking rain. However, anytime a big front moves through and soaks an area, be prepared to shoot.

Maryland has several dozen vista points, but not all of them inspire wonder. In fact, many are overgrown or just plain bad. There is no system or governing body that defines what a good vista is, but there are some obvious criteria, such as being high up and having a clear field of view. For the photographer, there are other things to look for before hauling gear to a location. I look for a clean foreground free of dead brush and make sure rocks have no graffiti. The middle ground must be clean and lush as well. There should be no clear-cuts or mines in view. A good vista should be inspiring and afford a large number of compositional possibilities. The best have a sublime quality that calls you back to them time and again.

I have attempted to include only the best Maryland has to offer. Certain measurements are important when selecting a shooting location. I've taken the following into account in compiling this guide:

Relief: The vertical distance from the edge of a vista to what's immediately below. For cliffs and ledges, the more the better. Ridges and hill tops may have no relief.

Elevation Difference: The vertical distance to the nearest low point of terrain.

Axis: The principal direction of the view, given in degrees (45°) or compass direction (northeast).

Field of View: The width of the visual field, given in degrees from left to right (90° to 160°).

Vistas also come in many types. The USGS recognizes a large number of names for different terrain features and high points. I've decided to use only the following four:

Cliff: Rock formation with large vertical relief where the terrain below falls away steeply. Typically cannot be climbed from below without special equipment and training.

Ledge: Rock formation with less vertical relief than a cliff, where the terrain does not fall away so steeply. Typically can be climbed from below without special equipment and training.

Cobble: A boulder field, boulder fall, talus slope, or patch of rock scree that forms an open area on a ridge crest or flank.

Ridge or summit: A location with no distinct edge that may or may not have vegetation cover.

Vistas and falls are rated on a 0 to 5 scale, where a 5 is a must-see location.

Photographing Waterfalls and Vistas

Amazing photographs can be made with even the simplest of cameras. What camera equipment to use is beyond the scope of this guide, but here are a few things to consider. Use a camera with a manual exposure setting capability that can shoot exposures of several seconds.

When shooting woodland scenes and waterfalls, pray for rain, fog, or mist. Shooting in bright sunlight is almost impossible. Overcast and flat lighting work best. If you can't shoot with the weather, wait for a cloud to soften the scene. Also throw water on rocks within a stream or near a fall. Even when it's overcast, rocks will render overly bright. Splash them with water to make them look better.

All of Maryland's vistas can be photographed at any time of day or season. Generally speaking, the best time of day for easterly facing vistas will be from one hour before sunrise to thirty minutes after; for westerly facing views, the best time is from thirty minutes before sunset to one hour after.

The most stunning vista point seasons are spring, during the latter portion of leaf out, and autumn, during peak color. Other good times are following a fresh snowfall or after large storms. Dramatic light will typically follow a clearing storm, and incredible skies will precede them, so keep an eye on the weather forecast and plan accordingly. I encourage you try and shoot moonrise and moonset during a full moon. At least once a month, moonrise will be within several minutes of sunset and vice versa. These are thrilling times to make photographs. With the newer generation of digital cameras, it's quite easy to photograph landscapes by moonlight when as little as half the moon is illuminated.

Vistas pose the added challenge of a sky that is much brighter than the foreground, typically by several stops. A graduated neutral density filter is an *essential* tool; buy a good one (more about that below). Because vistas have such a wide array of compositional possibilities, you'll end up using every lens you own, from an extreme wide-angle like a 17mm to a big telephoto like a 400mm, so bring them all. Put a polarizer on the camera and leave it on. Don't bother with a Skylight or UV filter—they're worthless. Warming filters will add color to sunrise and sunset skies, but don't overdo it. Don't use warming filters during the midday. Another handy filter to have is a 10CC magenta (the fluorescent mode in digital), which will enhance reds and pinks during twilight. Exposures longer than 1 second will be common at dusk and dawn, so a sturdy tripod that places the camera at eye level without extending the center post works best.

Helpful Hints

Photography means to paint with light, and good lighting should drive you when you shoot. You can take photographs at any hour of the day from any location, but there are some hints that will help you take more amazing shots:

- In the morning, start shooting before the sun comes up, and in the evening keep shooting after it goes down. Work the light until your camera can no longer provide exposure readings.
- Instead of shooting toward the sun, work with the light to your side or behind you. Sidelighting creates texture and shadows that separate hills and ridges, creating a three-dimensional effect. Side- and backlighting work especially well during fall.
- If there is thick cloud cover, be patient and wait for a "God beam"—a shaft of light through a hole in a cloud that spotlights the landscape. These are magical!
- Clearing and approaching storm fronts can create incredible cloud formations with magical colors like pink cotton candy. Keep abreast of changing weather patterns.
- Shoot every lens you own, starting with a wide-angle and finishing with a telephoto.
- Shoot until you run out of digital storage space or batteries.

Using a Graduated Filter

Although High Dynamic Range (HDR) merging software continues to get better, this postprocessing practice can be overdone. I still believe that a graduated neutral density filter is the most important tool to use when shooting vistas. This filter, which is gray on top and clear on the bottom, is used to even out or compensate exposures by darkening the sky so a scene can be recorded properly. They are either round, screw-type filters or square to allow for a changing horizon position. Get a square one with the appropriate filter mount for your camera. Cokin makes reasonably priced plastic sets. They also come in different intensities or shades of gray, listed as one-stop, two-stop, or three-stop filters, which darken the sky accordingly. I usually end up using a two-stop filter at dawn or dusk and a one-stop at midday. These filters also come in different edge types. A soft-edge filter has a smooth transition from clear to gray, whereas a hard-edge goes from clear to gray as a harsh line. I use both regularly.

To use a graduated filter, meter the foreground and record that value, then meter the sky near the horizon but not near the sun (the sun should never be part of a meter reading). Set your camera's exposure for the foreground reading, and then pick a graduated neutral density filter that will keep the sky at least one stop brighter than the foreground. In low or indirect light, such as from a twilight sky, use a gray card to meter the foreground. Bracket at least one stop on either side of what you expect, even when using digital cameras. Bracketing is cheap insurance.

Composition

The biggest issue with composition is where to put the horizon. It's usually not a good idea to place it in the middle of the frame. Generally, an image looks best when the horizon is placed in the top third of the frame. A basic premise of this idea is that you're photographing the landscape, not the sky, so don't include a lot of sky. But if the sky is where the magic is, then place the horizon in the bottom third of the frame. Whatever you do, just make sure the image looks balanced. It's also important to make sure the horizon is level.

I often see people come to a location, set up a tripod, shoot a couple frames, and then leave. They're really missing out, because the first view you see often isn't the best. Move left and right to change your perspective. Raise and lower your tripod. Get close to the edge, and then pull away. Put lots of foreground in the frame, and then none. Shoot every lens you own, beginning with a wide-angle and going longer and longer. Shoot twenty or thirty compositions from a location. Play with the scene until there is nothing left on your memory card.

Most important, always remember to take joy in the moment. The pressure to capture the flaming light of dawn can be overwhelming. Take time to step back from the camera and soak in the sublime. Taking the road less traveled is about the experience, not the images. Focus on the experience, and magical images will surely follow.

Footgear and Other Stuff

First, recognize this important fact: At some point you're going to get wet. Although you can get most anywhere with a good pair of sneakers, I don't recommend them. Ankle and arch support is very important when hiking along rocky trails, and boots that cover the ankle area are important. A twisted ankle is a common hiking injury, and as my own orthopedic surgeon will attest, you can break an ankle anywhere, at any time. Stout hightop boots are a must. When working in water use quality waders or heavy outdoor sandals, and don't forget mountain streams are ice cold.

You may want to attempt running some of these trails. Ironically enough, trail running is easier (at least for me) with very little support. I use a pair of Merrell Barefoot Zero Drop trail flats or Altra Zero Drop trail runners, and although I love my two pair of Vibrams, their rock plate isn't sufficient for trails like the AT.

Toting around thirty to fifty pounds of camera equipment is not always easy. I carry my gear in Lowepro camera backpacks. With a lighter complement of gear, use a waist pack or a big fanny pack. In any case, the object is to keep your hands free when walking on uneven terrain.

Hike 1 Bald Cypress Trail, Pocomoke River State Park, Worcester County

Type: walk	**Distance:** 1 mile
Rating: 3	**Time:** 30 minutes
GPS: 38° 7.332'N, 75° 29.747'W	**Elevation change:** 20 feet
Best time: any time	**Best lenses:** 20mm to 100mm
Difficulty: easy	

Directions: From the US-13/MD-12 interchange on the southeast side of Salisbury, take MD-12 south toward Snow Hill for 13.6 miles, then go right onto Nassa-wango Road. (MD-354 goes left.) In 6.8 miles, make a hard right onto River Road and enter Pocomoke State Park's Milburn Landing Area. Continue on River Road for 1.3 miles and park in the large boat/trail parking lot. GPS coordinates: 38° 7.332'N, 75° 29.747'W.

Pocomoke State Park and Pocomoke State Forest run for quite a distance along the Pocomoke River. The park is divided by the river, with the Shad Landing Area on the east bank and the Milburn Landing Area on the west. US-113 flanks the east side and MD-364 the west with the core of the park running from Snow Hill at the north end and Pocomoke City at the south end.

Bald Cypress Trail. When shooting glassy calm water always look for complete reflections. The inky black water acts like a mirror, and even a polarizer couldn't penetrate the surface. *Canon EOS 5D Mkii, Canon 20-105L, Polarizer, ISO100 setting, f5.6 @ .3s*

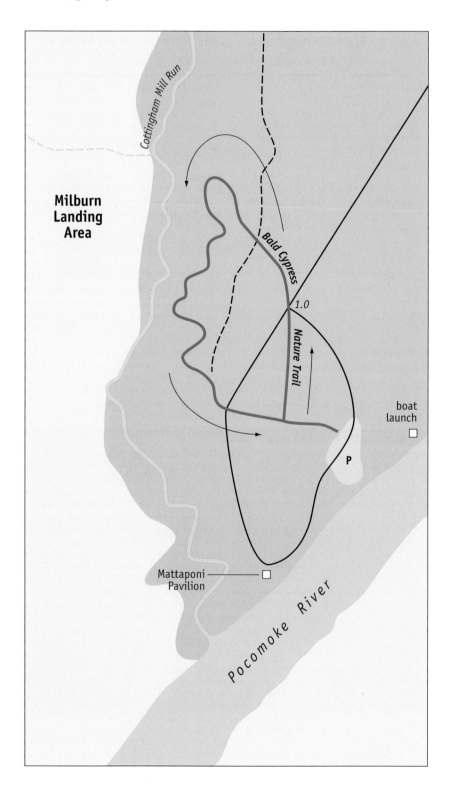

Milburn
Landing
Area

Cottingham Mill Run

Bald Cypress

1.0

Nature Trail

boat
launch

P

Mattaponi
Pavilion

Pocomoke River

This short trail through dense forest is a quick bit of fun. It's a good starter hike for kids. It's short, has some interesting birds, a few frogs and lizards, and—most important of all—an ample supply of mud to fling at your little brother or sister. From the parking area, walk past the large descriptive sign and follow a wide, white-blazed path, turning right when you come to an arrow. In .1 miles, cross the access to Mattaponi Pavilion, and then at .13 miles cross a yellow-blazed woods road—just stick to the white blazes.

Around .15 miles, the trail swings left to run beside Cottingham Mill Run, a slack backwater tributary filled with intensely green mosses and sedges. At .4 miles, follow a blue arrow to a little viewing platform or landing that juts into the run. Set up your tripod and blast away, because this is a delightfully intimate scenic location.

Return to the main trail following the arrow right. The trail swings left away from the run at .55 miles, after which you immediately arrive at an arrow right, taking you back toward Mattaponi Road. In a dozen yards, cross the road about 100 yards away from the gate near River Road at .7 miles. Rejoin the main access trail at .85 miles and bear right to return to your car at 1 mile.

Hike 2 **Milburn Landing Trail, Pocomoke State Forest, Worcester County**

Type: hike	**Distance:** 3.6 miles
Rating: 4	**Time:** 1 hour, 30 minutes
GPS: 38° 7.653'N, 75° 29.391'W	**Elevation change:** 100 feet
Best time: any time	**Best lenses:** 20mm to 100mm
Difficulty: easy	

Directions: See page 17. After entering Pocomoke State Park's Milburn Landing Area, continue on River Road for .8 miles and turn left on the day-use area entrance road. Park along the road just past the entrance station where a woods road crosses. GPS coordinates: 38° 7.653'N, 75° 29.391'W.

Head downhill away from the road (northeast), following a wide, red-blazed trail. In about 500 feet, come to a triad-shaped junction. To the right is your return route, to the left a cutoff trail, and straight is the path you'll follow now. Continue ahead, passing a cemetery at .22 miles, through an open grassy area where the trail becomes a road, and arrive at a T at .45 miles. Turn left, looking for red plastic stake-type blazes. The unblazed cutoff joins from the left at .55 miles. There will be an arrow with a number 8 on it pointing right.

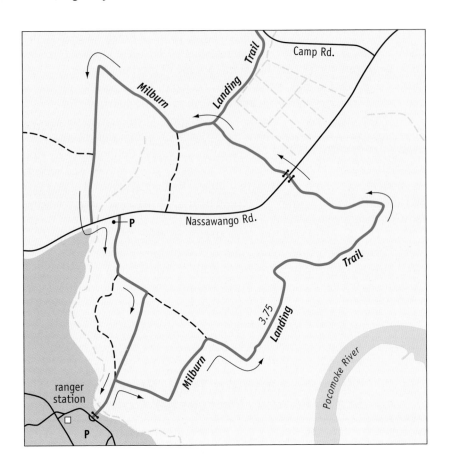

Pass a gate at .74 miles as you approach Nassawango Road and go left to walk along the road into sparse but fast-moving oncoming traffic. In less than 100 yards go right onto another woods road at .8 miles, marked by an open area and a red plastic stake near two closely spaced pines. The lane you'll walk down has forest service yellow boundary paint on some trees; another nearby lane has private land white paint and an old telephone pole at the end with "2W ABC" in white lettering at the bottom.

Moving quickly on the lonely woods lane, pass a useless green gate near 1.0 mile; another old road merges at an acute angle from the left. Continue ahead, moving almost due north near the state forest boundary and the eastern edge of a young stand of pine trees. At 1.3 miles T into another woods road and go right to follow red plastic stake blazes. Whether you're moving quickly or slowly, keep a very sharp eye out at 1.6 miles for a left turn off the woods road onto a foot path. Even though it is marked by a large red arrow, I missed this turn and ended up near Nassawango Road before I realized what had happened—that made for a .7 mile detour that I wasn't in the mood for.

Having successfully made the left turn onto the narrower footpath, you've entered what can best be described as lumpy terrain, which will slow your pace. However, it's a delightful forest trail, so I didn't mind breaking from my light jog into a slow meander. After about 100 yards of deep soil, T into yet another woods road at 1.73 miles and bear right. Cross Nassawango Road again at 2.0 miles and pass into a dense pine stand that gives way to hardwoods as the road smoothes out somewhat. T into yet another woods road at 2.33 miles. Left is unmarked and right is your red blaze—go right.

The now wide, straight road swings left toward the river, then makes a slow right, climbing gently at 2.6 miles to make a long, looping left back to the river where you'll hit another T at 2.78 miles. Go right. Finally, make your next-to-last turn by going right at 3.03 miles and head along the woods road to the last T at 3.15 miles. Go left, returning to your car at 3.8 miles. Phew, that's a lot of T's.

Hike 3 — Tarr Tract Bike Trails, Pocomoke State Forest, Worcester County

Type: hike	**Distance:** 2.6 miles
Rating: 3	**Time:** 50 minutes
GPS: 38° 7.124'N, 75° 28.054'W	**Elevation change:** 100 feet
Best time: any time	**Best lenses:** 20mm to 100mm
Difficulty: easy	

Directions: See page 17. From the US-13/MD-12 interchange on the southeast side of Salisbury, take MD-12 south for 14.8 miles into Snow Hill. Just after crossing the Pocomoke River, turn right onto Market Street, then in .2 miles go left on Church Street, all the while following signs for MD-12. Take Church Street out of town for 1.5 miles until you hit US-113. Go right onto US-113 south and in 5.6 miles you'll come to a tan building on the right. Turn right onto Blades Road. Park on the left in a sandy lane in .3 miles, without blocking the gate. GPS coordinates: 38° 7.124'N, 75° 28.054'W.

The Tarr Tract Bike Trails are a network of three loops with spur trails to US-113. This access point on Blades Road eliminates some tight parking and is also much quieter. This 2.6-mile loop combines the northern yellow section with the southern green section to form one big loop.

Normally I walk with a GPS on my shoulder, but after shooting from well before sunrise at Assateague (see Hike 6) I decided to go for a little trail run to stretch my legs. If you've read my other books, you know I really love to

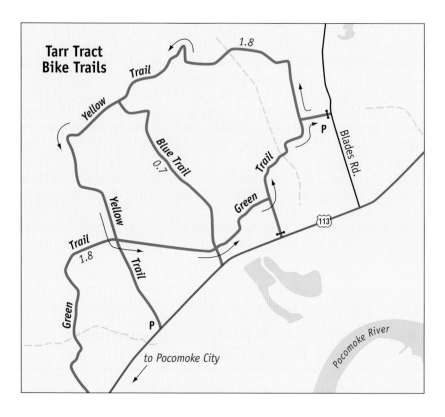

hike; trail running is somewhat new and I've come to enjoy it immensely as a contemplative exercise. The Tarr Tract is off the beaten path, and it's pretty and relatively free of ankle hazards, so feel free to lace 'em up and crank out some miles.

Begin by heading 100 yards down the wide sandy lane to the Y and bear right on the yellow-blazed trail. At .3 miles the trail swings left, and near .5 miles makes a poorly marked hard left. The blue trail T's in from the left at .7 miles. Continue straight on the yellow-blazed trail

For the next .5 miles the route is fairly straight before it makes a casual sweep left at 1.2 miles to run south toward US-113. The green trail is found at 1.63 miles, where you make a hard left at a well-blazed intersection. From here back to the car the trail is well groomed and you can really push a speed workout if you want. Cross the blue-blazed trail again at 2.0 miles and slowly lose the sound of US-113 as the trail works away from it. Go left when you hit a T at 2.25 miles, then come a few more minor, but poorly marked, jogs before returning to the head of the loop at 2.6 miles. Finally, turn right for the final 100 yards back to your car.

If you plan on shooting, the best spot is the manicured pine grove you went by in the first one-third mile. The ordered rows make for nice graphic lines, the uniform browse line makes an interesting false horizon, and this is a killer location in fog. Imagine a uniform formation of trees fading from an extremely detailed foreground tree to a monochrome background element. Soft focus would be perfect in that situation—talk about an artsy contrast study. Now I'm kind of bummed I had clear weather.

Hike 4 **Marsh Overlook Trail, Chincoteague National Wildlife Refuge, Accomack County, Virginia**

Type: walk	**Distance:** .8 miles
Rating: 4	**Time:** 30 minutes
GPS: 37° 54.643'N, 75° 20.995'W	**Elevation change:** none
Best time: early morning through late afternoon	**Best lenses:** 20mm to 200mm
Difficulty: easy	

Directions: From the US-13/US113 interchange south of Pocomoke City, take US-13 south for 8.6 miles and then turn left onto VA-175, following signs for Chincoteague and NASA Wallops Island. In 10.9 miles cross from the bridge over the channel onto Chincoteague Island, continue straight on Maddox Street for 1.1 miles, and carefully make your way through the roundabout following signs for the refuge. Continue along Beach Access Road for a total of 1.2 miles, crossing the Assateague Channel onto the refuge proper, and finally turn left onto the Wildlife Loop access road. Park in the large parking area on the left for the Marsh Trail and Wildlife Loop. GPS coordinates: 37° 54.643'N, 75° 20.995'W.

Chincoteague is famous for its ponies, but I prefer the landscape opportunities more. The gate to the refuge opens at 6:00 A.M. most of the year and 5:00 A.M. May through September. Closing times vary with season and sometimes with weather, so check the website:www.fws.gov/northeast/chinco/. Cost is $8 per car per day, with seasonal passes available. None of the trails are accessible without passing through the fee station. The 25mph speed limit is strictly enforced to protect the endangered Delmarva fox squirrel. Unlike your average backyard gray squirrel, the Delmarva subspecies is no sprinter and isn't fast enough to outrun any vehicle. It is very important that you drive cautiously. Also, don't even think about approaching the ponies. They aren't tame by any means, and a kick from a horse will put you in the hospital for a long time—just ask my grandfather.

The Wildlife Loop can be closed to cars for a number of reasons. During my April trip it opened at 3:00 P.M. for recreational bike use and foot traffic; however, the Marsh Trail is a better choice, because pavement is not an ideal hiking surface.

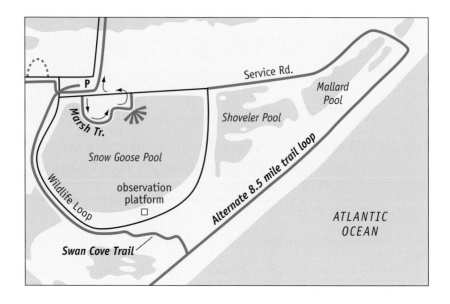

Follow the boardwalk away from the parking area to the Marsh View overlook. After a few dozen yards, cross Wildlife Drive and continue ahead on the Marsh Trail. Arrive at a footbridge at .12 miles, which provides a nice landscape view looking along 75°. In spring, the full green foliage of the marshland is scenic, and in autumn, the few deciduous trees add enough fall color to make an early morning shot well worth your time.

The trail swings left in a northerly direction, following the crest of a dike. Water is both left and right, and wild horses do frequent the trail, as evidenced by a pile of fresh manure I had to sidestep on my hike. That's when a pony emerged from some heavy grass and stood firmly in my path. Keeping as much distance as my wide-angle allowed, about 20 feet, I framed the piebald animal against a blue sky and discovered I had dead batteries. Don't let this happen to you! Always bring spares.

Continue along to the view platform, which is at .54 miles, close to where the footpath links up with the Wildlife Loop north of the parking lot. Overlooking a shallow wetland low tide will expose hundreds of yards of mud. Look for graphic patterns of ripples and tributary channels that snake through the dark brown marsh bottom. The view is truly panoramic, so take some time to stitch together wide angle and telephoto versions, the best spanning from 65° to 210°.

As I sat pondering the implications of a particularly dark cloud mass to my south, an avocet wheeled a series of ever tighter turns before landing a dozen yards away, still too far for the lens I had. Avocets are fascinating birds to watch. When in flocks, they congregate in close quarters as they forage the mudflats like grazing sheep. On the wing, they form a mat of solid avian carpet a few feet above the water. Flocks numbering in the hundreds will turn in unison and when they do their color instantly changes depending on whether you see the top side or belly. It is a hypnotic dance of color flickering from white to brown and back again every couple of seconds. One time at Bombay Hook NWR in Delaware a harrier sprinted into a large flock, hoping for a quick meal, only to find itself being chased by an irate bald eagle. The avocet flock cleaved evenly, the two halves wheeling violently, their white tops flipping to tan and back as fast as I've ever seen. The harrier, now flummoxed, decided it was more important to outrun the eagle, which was now within a yard of its tail, when it popped up into a stall and began its well-known hover. The eagle, not being as agile, made a frustrated cry and looped away from both the now-wading avocet flock and hovering harrier to pass within a dozen yards of my position. None of it was captured on film, but that's okay—had I been intent on the shot, I would have missed the whole thing. The lesson here is to not let the camera interfere with a moment of awe. Sit, watch, experience, and then grab the camera.

You'll T into the Wildlife Loop at .65 miles and go left (south) on the paved road to return to your car, which you'll get back to at .8 miles.

Hike 5 Woodland Trail, Chincoteague National Wildlife Refuge, Accomack County, Virginia

Type: walk	Distance: 2.75 miles
Rating: 5	Time: 1 hour
GPS: 37° 53.749'N, 75° 21.683'W	Elevation change: none
Best times: early morning through late afternoon	Best lenses: 20mm to 200mm
Difficulty: easy	

Directions: See page 23. After making your way through the roundabout, continue along Beach Access Road for a total of 2.7 miles, crossing the Assateague Channel onto the refuge proper, and finally turn right into the signed Woodland Trail parking area. GPS coordinates: 37° 53.749'N, 75° 21.683'W.

Follow the paved path away from the parking area, and at the Y bear right to begin the loop. Passing through a loblolly stand, the wide path makes for fast walking; if you're jogger, this is the place to lace up your shoes and stretch your legs. At .51 miles come to a boardwalk on the right that takes you to Pony View. The platform was built in 1999 by the service project arm of Elderhostel. In front of you is an open marsh with the lighthouse lantern visible above the trees. To the left, you can see the houses and condos on Chincoteague Island.

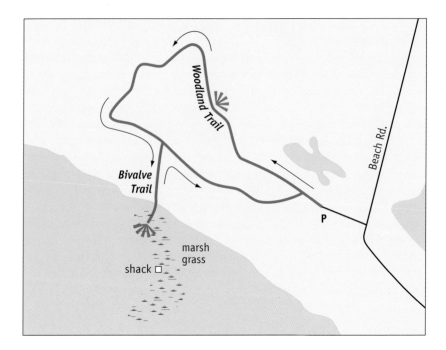

Head back to the path and at .74 miles bear right onto a sandy footpath, which drops you a few feet to a fence line separating the woods from the marsh. You're now facing a small copse of trees where ponies like to hang out to avoid the midday sun. At 1.1 miles a sandy road cuts off to the right at an acute angle, leading to a closed area, so stick with the paved path ahead. When you get to the Bivalve Trail, an oyster shell-covered path at 1.3 miles, go right and arrive at the water's edge, now at 1.45 miles. In front of you is an old oysterman's shack, which is now home to a large osprey nest. The nest is about 100 yards away, so unless you have a massive lens, like an 800mm, just have a seat and enjoy watching osprey hunt the shallows. Clearly visible to the right is NASA's Wallops Island facility. The view is more or less south, and the field of view spans from due east to west. The old shack and pilings provide the best shooting opportunities the trail has to offer. You can also wander along the marsh up to a hundred yards left or right, exploring for more things to photograph. As you head right, you'll encounter a large aluminum retro-reflector aimed at Wallops Island. I don't know what purpose it serves—perhaps it's a distance-ranging calibration target.

When you're done, head back along the Bivalve Trail to the main trail, turn right to continue the loop, and return to your car, arriving at 2.75 miles. I found the trail to be quiet except for the bicycle riders near the beginning. It was apparent that many of the kids I saw don't get outside much, even the teenagers. In an age of perpetual screen time, I think it's important to get kids into the "woods" as often as possible. After all, you don't need 3D glasses here.

Hike 6	**Assateague Island National Seashore, Wicomico County**	

Type: walk	**Best time:** sunrise or sunset
Rating: 5	**Difficulty:** easy
GPS: 38° 12.403'N, 75° 9.628'W	**Distance:** 1.75 miles
38° 12.029'N, 75° 9.795'W	**Time:** 2 hours
38° 11.870'N, 75° 9.483'W	**Elevation change:** none
38° 11.431'N, 75° 9.593'W	**Best lenses:** 20mm to 400mm

Directions: From the US-13/US-50 bypass interchange on the east side of Salisbury, take US-50 (Ocean Gateway) east toward Ocean City for 17.9 miles to US-113 just north of Berlin. Exit onto US-113 south toward Berlin, and in 1.5 miles turn left onto MD-376 at a gas station on the near left. Follow MD-376 for 4.1 miles and turn right on MD-611. MD-611 will make a long sweeping left to head east for the island. Make a hard right before entering the state park, and after a total of 4.3 miles turn right onto Bayside Drive at signs for Life of the Marsh Trail. Park in the large lot on the left. GPS coordinates: 38° 12.403'N, 75° 9.628'W.

Assateague National Seashore is a U.S. fee area. Access from Maryland is $15.00 per car and is good for seven days. If you're going to be stopping here, or at Chincoteague or Bombay Hook, I recommend the National Parks/Federal Lands Pass. It costs $80.00, is good for one year, and can be used at every federal fee area.

There are a great many ponies on this end of the island. They may look tame but they aren't. In the spring, the mares will be protective of their foals and in the fall, the stallions are territorial and just plain old mean. Give all animals you find a wide berth.

This driving and walking tour hits the highlights. After exploring, find a nice spot, pick your light, and relax. There's no rush—the place isn't going anywhere.

This short, .5-mile, handicap-accessible boardwalk loop is a good sunrise location. You'll find habituated plovers and limpkins plying the shallows near the boardwalk, so bring your biggest lenses. There are many pull-offs with very informative signs that make for convenient spots to set up a tripod. There's an overlook platform at .31 miles with a set of stairs that drop you to a west-facing marsh with an inviting sandy beach that wraps around you to form a large cove. From here, sunset options are endless.

Continue the loop back to the car and head for Ferry Landing, which is .5 miles south, and park at the road's end. GPS coordinates: 38° 12.029'N, 75° 9.795'W. There's a short boardwalk that also provides expansive west-facing views. Now head back toward the main road and turn right, then pull over on the right in the signed parking area for Life of the Forest Trail. GPS coordinates: 38° 11.870'N, 75° 9.483'W.

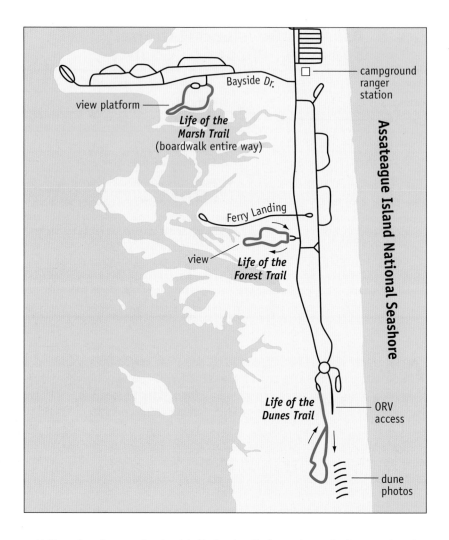

Follow the signs to begin this little .5-mile loop through the woods. The loop takes you through a loblolly stand with some nice intimate, graphic scenes. There are overlapping branches, engorged male cones in April, lichens, and interesting bark patterns. However, head for the overlook, which has a nice view of the marsh. The principle view is westerly, spanning from 172° to 292°. Foreground shrubs will need to be fully green to look comfortable in the bottom of your frame. Prior to May, the entire landscape will be monochrome tan.

Head back to the main road and follow it to the end of the parking lot for the Life of the Dunes Trail, which is to the right of the ORV access. GPS coordinates: 38° 11.431′N, 75° 9.593′W.

Head south from the lot following the signs and make a slow turn of the .75-mile loop. Signs along the way describe vegetation and wildlife habitats.

Assateague Dunes Trail. Shooting need not end after the sun goes down. When you have a white surface, it will reflect the sky's subtle pastel tones. After shooting a few frames, don't forget to move your feet to explore the entire scene. *Canon EOS 5D Mkii, Canon 20-105L, Polarizer, ISO100 setting, f22 @ .8s*

Assateague Marsh Trail. On the one or two days a month when moonrise coincides with sunset, you should be in the field shooting. These trips need to be preplanned to get the most benefit of your valuable time. *Canon EOS 5D Mkii, Canon 20-105L, 2 stop graduate, ISO800 setting, f8 @ 1/25s*

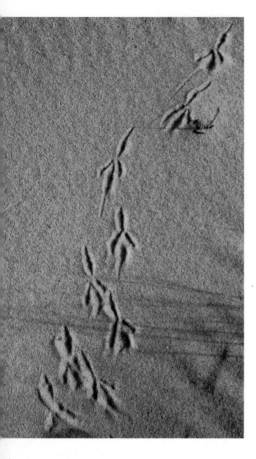

Assateague Dunes Trail. Patterns in the sand make for wonderful little graphic compositions. I have no idea what bird this may have been, only that it was quite small. *Canon EOS 5D Mkii, Canon 20-105L, Polarizer, ISO100 setting, f22 @ .5s*

Your spot is about 250 yards in and to the east along the dune line guarding the beach. Here you'll find firm sand to walk on and, more importantly, those gorgeous ripples and dune grass circles fabricated by the ever-present wind.

I shot these by twilight so the sun would create shadow texture; then after dark I shot stars. It was incredible until I got lost heading back to my car. Although my GPS pointed the correct way, the wind-driven sand filled my headlight beam like snowfall and my numerous diversions kept dead ending among the trees. So I stopped to relax, headed for the ocean where the footing was better, and followed the reflective ORV markers back to the parking lot. It was a gorgeous night so I didn't mind the hour's diversion. Fortunately I had water with me—hiking through sand is extremely hard!

Hike 7 Fairmount Wildlife Management Area, Somerset County

Type: walk	**Difficulty:** easy
Rating: 5+	**Distance:** 4.15 miles
GPS: 38° 4.725'N, 75° 49.876'W	**Time:** 2 hours, 30 minutes
38° 5.244'N 75°, 48.419'W	**Elevation change:** none
Best time: sunrise or sunset	**Best lenses:** 20mm to 400mm

Directions: From the south end of the US-13 bypass around Salisbury, take US-13 (Ocean Highway) south for 12.2 miles and bear right onto MD-413 following signs for Crisfield. In 1.3 miles turn off MD-413 south onto MD-361 west; there will be an equipment shed or repair shop on the left as you turn. Take MD-361 through Upper Fairmount and Fairmount, and bear right onto Ford Wharf Road. (There may be a sign for the WMA.) Park in a large gravel lot with hard edges and set your parking brake. GPS coordinates: 38° 5.072'N, 75° 49.700'W.

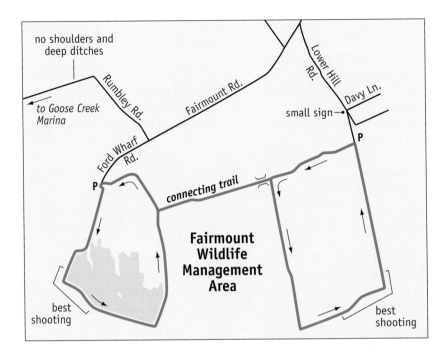

The roads along MD-361 after the village of Upper Fairmount have soft shoulders or water-filled ditches on both sides, so take great care anywhere in and around the WMA. Just look for the bayou-style burial vaults in the church yards and you'll understand how high the water table is.

This level, 1.9-mile loop atop an impoundment dike makes a circuit of the West Impoundment. Walk past the yellow gate and turn right toward the bay. The section from here through the first two lefts, about 1 mile total, covers the west and south sides and is photographically

Fairmount WMA East Impoundment. It took a long time—and some very muddy knees—to get this foreground and the thin arm of grass on the right to settle into a pleasing shape. My lens is about 20 inches above the grass, and I had to move every thirty seconds to keep the sun at the end of the grassy arm. Always be aware of how fast the sun moves along the horizon during dawn and dusk. Canon EOS 5D Mkii, Canon 20-105L, 2 stop graduate, ISO100 setting, f16 @ 1/4s

the best here. On the southwest corner you're closest to the bay and can step off the dike into the marshlands. Hiking boots are okay if you're careful, but hip or chest waders provide the best protection, especially if you're kneeling to shoot foregrounds. You can shoot wildlife, full panoramic scenes, moonlit landscapes, clouds, or anything you can imagine with abandon. Just take care when pointing any lens north that you don't have the big blue water tank in frame. Finish the loop back to the car and head for the east impoundment.

Head back east on MD-361 for .9 miles and turn right onto Lower Hill Road. Follow the narrow road for .5 miles and bear right at a Y marked with a tiny yellow sign when you come even with Davy Lane; there'll be a white mailbox on the left. Follow the narrow gravel lane through the trees, park in the gravel and grass parking area between the gates, and set the parking brake. GPS coordinates: 38° 5.244'N, 75° 48.419'W.

This 2.25-mile loop around the east impoundment also follows a dike, but the impoundment is not as open as the west one. In this case, the best bet is to head directly for the southeast corner of the impoundment by heading due south around the left gate and speed-walking the route for .7 miles. This

Fairmount WMA East Impoundment. When scouting this location the day before, I settled on this human effigy-like cluster of grass which I came to call "Burning Man." Shot from the impoundment's southeast corner a few steps off the dike, I had to be very careful since a deep canal sat just behind me. *Canon EOS 5D Mkii, Canon 20-105L, 2 stop graduate, ISO100 setting, f16 @ 1/4s*

corner and the couple hundred yards of dike to the north and west have the best wildlife and landscape shooting. The eastward view at dawn is better here than at any other spot along the impoundment's entire south side. However, if you've only got one shot at sunrise, I'd go for the east impoundment's southwest corner. The deep canal, calm eastward view into the pool, and moonset exposure provides the best options.

If you have time, head for the Goose Creek Marina by heading back toward the west impoundment and turning right onto Rumbley Road. Follow Rumbley Road for 2.2 miles (bearing right toward Frenchtown) and go right onto the unsigned Claude Hall Road to the wharf. There are several working boats, lots of crab pots, and fishing gear in large piles. You can work nifty graphic patterns of tangled ropes, colorful crab pot floats, and such. Don't be surprised if you get some stares, and don't forget to respectfully ask for permission whenever photographing people.

Hike 8 Deal Island Wildlife Management Area, Somerset County

Type: walk	Difficulty: easy
Rating: 5+	Distance: 4.15 miles
GPS: 38° 10.432'N 75° 52.838'W	Time: 2 hours, 30 minutes
38° 9.247'N 75° 54.441'W	Elevation change: none
Best time: sunrise or sunset	Best lenses: 20mm to 400mm

Directions: From the south end of the US-13 bypass around Salisbury, take US-13 (Ocean Highway) south for 7.3 miles and bear right onto MD-363 west (Deal Island Road) in the town of Princess Anne. In 9.2 miles bear left onto the gravel Game Reserve Road that seems to disappear into the marsh. In 1 mile, park near the gate without blocking access for other vehicles and set the parking brake. GPS coordinates: 38° 10.432'N, 75° 52.838'W.

The roads along MD-363 after leaving Princess Anne have soft shoulders or water-filled ditches on both sides, so take great care anywhere in and around the WMA. Look for prepared or paved pullouts and signed parking areas when pulling off the road.

As you head down Game Reserve Road, the phragmites alongside give way to open marsh and you begin to get a sense of how enormous Deal Island actually is. The property is 13,000 acres, and this driving/walking tour gives you a good look at the 2,800-acre central impoundment of Dames Quarter Marsh. The biggest mistake I made in coming here was not bringing a bike or my running shoes. The 9.8-mile dike system loop around the impoundment is simply too big to walk with a decent load of camera gear. Here are a couple short out-and-back walks to wet your whistle. There are other trail and dike systems to the north off of Drawbridge Road and to the north and west off Deal Island Road. All have signed parking areas, but none have the expansive views and habitat that the Dames Quarter Marsh does.

From the gate, head west along the closed road away from the boat ramp for maybe a half mile. This drier section of marsh has a checkerboard pattern of inches-deep ditches, almost like a rice paddy. You'll find one or two picnic tables along the way, and the ever-present sound of flies hovering close to the ground fills the air. This is not a place to be in July; the cooler weather from late October to April would be best. The marsh is a carpet of short green grass and the flat uniformity of the landscape isn't very photogenic. You'll need interesting clouds to work this location, placing the horizon near the frame's bottom third to emphasize how lonely the place looks. You can continue for about .7 miles from the car, passing through a stand of trees, to get to the WMA parking area off Deal Island Road just west of Messick Road.

Head back to your car, take Game Reserve Road back to MD-363, and make the hard left to head west. Take MD-363 west for 2.1 miles and turn left onto Riley Roberts Road. There's a large tan house on the left and a red brick church about 100 yards away on the right up MD-363. Riley Roberts

Deal Island. I had shot several images near the boat launch and the water control structure, and as I was heading back to my campsite I noticed this island-like meander. The only way to get the shot was to climb atop my Jeep. *Canon EOS 5D Mkii, Canon 20-105L, 2 stop graduate, ISO800 setting, f16 @ 3.2s*

Road makes several blockish turns before becoming a gravel dike top road at the WMA border. Park here (GPS coordinates: 38° 10.492′N, 75° 54.671′W) for a few moments before continuing. You're at the extreme western corner of the impoundment and 1.65 miles west of your last parking spot. The path you followed previously went northwest toward the highway, then saw-toothed back southwest before hitting the impoundment, where it then ran west to this spot, a walking distance of 2.3 miles. The view into the impoundment is southeast, and to get sufficient relief you'll need to climb onto the roof of your car.

Now head south along the road to the large gavel parking area at the boat ramp, 1.6 miles away. Here's your spot. The boat ramp and dock provide a nice open location for shooting and there are also views facing west from farther off the road. Look for some lovely full-circle meanders in the marsh. You can walk east from the ramp as far as you'd like; the water control structure over Big Sound Creek is nice. Be careful when crossing the scaffold atop it— it's some very deep water and the tidal current could pin you to the sluices. I went for a total of a mile east and the whole time just couldn't pick a spot because it's all so nice. In the end, I settled for the boat ramp area because the bulkhead provided enough relief to get the shot I was looking for.

I can't say enough about Deal Island. I wish I had more time to explore at twilight and to shoot by full moonlight. More importantly, I wish I could have gotten there in late October when the place is lousy with ducks and geese. But, with the aftereffects of Superstorm Sandy still being felt, I'll have to leave a multi-day exploration of Deal Island for another time.

Hike 9 **Roaring Point Park, Wicomico County**

Type: walk	**Distance:** .2 miles
Rating: 3	**Time:** 10 minutes
GPS: 38° 16.011'N 75° 54.773'W	**Elevation change:** none
Best times: sunrise or sunset	**Best lenses:** 20mm to 100mm
Difficulty: easy	

Directions: From US-50 north of Salisbury, take US-50 east into Salisbury (don't get on the bypass, which loops east of town). From the bypass cutoff, continue for 2.5 miles and turn right on MD-349 south (Nanticoke Road). MD-349 will eventually swing southward, and after a total of 20.2 miles turn right at a three-prong intersection onto Red Hill Road; there'll be a small sign for the park. Park at the road's end in the gravel parking lot. GPS coordinates: 38° 16.011'N, 75° 54.773'W.

A level trail of about 100 yards drops onto a glorious bayside beach. To your right is little Naticoke Harbor, and just under a half mile to the left is Roaring Point, where you can shoot west-facing panoramic shots. Across the Naticoke River are Fishing Bay WMA and Elliot Island. Just beyond that is Blackwater NWR. I didn't bother bringing my camera, although this is a great location, but instead slipped off my boots and flopped onto the sand to soak my tired feet. You should do the same.

Ellis Bay WMA is to the south, and access there is much harder than at Deal Island and Fairmount WMA farther south, so don't bother trying to work at Ellis Bay. However, I do recommend a side trip to the village of White

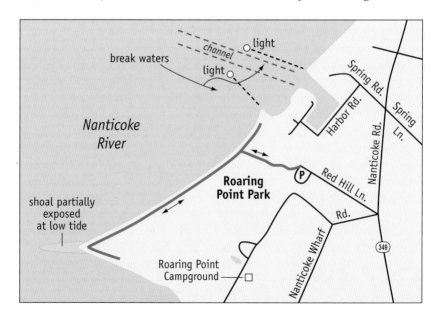

Haven to the east off of MD-352. White Haven is the northern ferry terminus for the Wicomico River ferry that connects Princess Anne with direct route to the villages of Bivalve and Nanticoke. The little colonial-era town has maybe thirty buildings and a small eight-room inn, the White Haven Hotel. This little town is picturesque, quaint, and just a neat place to wander for an hour.

Hike 10 Key Wallace Trail, Blackwater National Wildlife Refuge, Dorchester County

Type: walk	**Distance:** 3 miles
Rating: 4+	**Time:** 1 hour, 20 minutes
GPS: 38° 26.936'N, 76° 5.824'W	**Elevation change:** none
Best time: early morning through late afternoon	**Best lenses:** 20mm to 200mm
Difficulty: easy	

Directions: From the intersection of US-50 and MD-16 on the eastern side of Cambridge, take MD-16 west for 7.3 miles, then go left on MD-335 (Golden Hill Road). In 3.9 miles turn left at a Y onto Key Wallace Drive. There'll be a brown/white sign for Blackwater marking the turn. In 2.2 miles park on the left in a large, shaded gravel parking area on the left where Egypt Road continues left and Key Wallace makes a right to head into the refuge. GPS coordinates: 38° 26.936'N, 76° 5.824'W.

NOTE: Roads south and east off the refuge through Fishing Bay WMA are only inches above sea level and parking on the shoulder is not recommended. If you decide to take a driving tour south out of the refuge across Maple Dam Road toward Andrews and MD-336, use only the gravel or oyster shell-paved pullouts. Also, the road has sharp curves and if you're preoccupied with the view through the windshield you're in for an expensive towing bill. If you head east on Griffith Neck Road and south on Elliot Island Road toward Elliot it's the same; about 6 miles of Elliot Island Road had very soft shoulders or none at all. There is a "scary" hog-backed bridge at a place called Gray's Marsh that's fairly photogenic. However, I encourage you to go all the way out to the village of Elliot and Wharf Road to photograph the working boats at the small dock at the road's end—the afternoon light here is magical.

Blackwater NWR is huge but hiking opportunities are minimal. The refuge is geared more toward auto tourism than foot traffic. The gate to Wildlife Drive is automatic and in prime fall season it opens at dawn. Cost is $3 per car and $1 for bikes and pedestrians.

Walk up to the map kiosk and note that the trail is divided into red and blue sections. In the fall, various trails will be closed for deer hunting, but not on Sundays. Check with the refuge for seasons and closures. This trail heads out into an "upland" forest rather than toward the marshlands along the bay. "Upland" here means its elevation is about 7 feet.

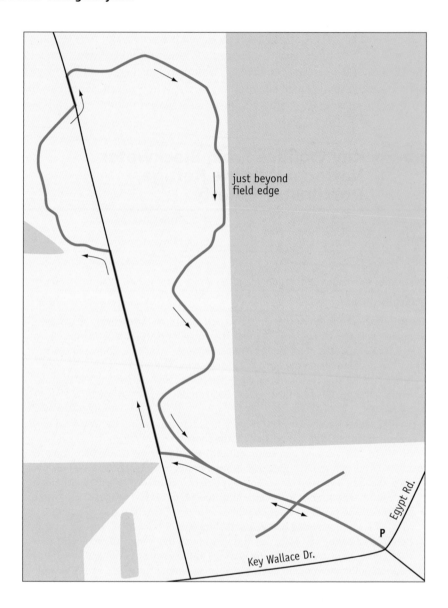

just beyond
field edge

Egypt Rd.

P

Key Wallace Dr.

It's a straight .28-mile walk along a quiet, tree-lined trail to a signed divide for the blue and yellow trail sections. Bear left onto the yellow section. At .36 miles arrive at a T with a woods road and turn right. You'll arrive at two pools at .56 miles. There's a hunter parking area, and nearby are two red-capped wells of some kind. Continue ahead along the road, then depart the road by turning left at a large yellow arrow at .8 miles. Yellow signs, blazes, and arrows mark the route, although some are hard to see in autumn as they blend in with the fall colors. The trail makes several hard jogs, so keep a keen eye for blazes and make use of the occasional benches to sit and absorb the woods.

Rejoin the road at 1.3 miles where the yellow trail goes to the right, making for a quick return to your car. The blue trail goes to the left, taking you deeper into the woods, so go left. In several dozen yards, go right at a blue arrow at 1.4 miles. At 1.5 miles arrive at a blue post in the midst of a confusing intersection of game trails and sandy-bottomed water channels. Bear right to about 10 o'clock and look for the next post about 40 yards away, hidden by a group of three trees. A short while later, the trail swings hard right at 1.7 miles to come parallel with a field on your left, about 50 yards away through the trees. Meandering to and fro, the blue trail can be challenging to keep, so walk slowly. After a delightful stroll, return to the Y you passed earlier at 2.5 miles and bear left to return to your car.

Since it was early deer season, the first day of November duck season, and Canada goose migrant and resident season, I opted for an orange ensemble for my hikes in and around Blackwater. As I returned to my muddy jeep, an older couple was getting out of their Lexus, he in firmly pressed kakis and she in upscale skirt and open-toed sandals with a designer handbag. By way of hello, the woman remarked, "My, you're dressed rather brightly." I replied that I didn't want to get shot. This stopped her in her tracks. I told them about the current seasons, looked at the woman, and said, "That's why you can hear all that gunfire coming from the marshes for the past few hours." "Oh," she said, "I thought it was fireworks or something." Her husband's head spun so fast I swear I could hear his neck crack. It was one of my funnier exchanges in writing this guide. They opted to get back in their car.

Hike 11 Marsh Edge, Blackwater National Wildlife Refuge, Dorchester County

Type: walk	Distance: 0.3 miles
Rating: 3	Time: 20 minutes
GPS: 38° 26.410'N, 76° 5.460'W	Elevation change: none
Best time: early morning through late afternoon	Best lenses: 20mm to 200mm
Difficulty: easy	

Directions: From the intersection of US-50 and MD-16 on the eastern side of Cambridge, take MD-16 west for 7.3 miles, then go left on MD-335 (Golden Hill Road). In 3.9 miles turn left at a Y onto Key Wallace Drive; there'll be a brown/white sign for Blackwater marking the turn. In 2.2 miles turn right to stay on Key Wallace Drive where Egypt Road continues left, then in .4 miles go right onto Wildlife Drive. Go through the gate, bear left onto the Marsh Edge Trail access road in .3 miles and park in the large signed parking area. GPS coordinates: 38° 26.410'N, 76° 5.460'W.

Blackwater NWR is huge but hiking opportunities are minimal. The refuge is geared more toward auto tourism then it is to foot traffic. The gate to Wildlife Drive is automatic and in prime fall season it opens at dawn. Cost is $3 per car, $1 for bikes and pedestrians.

The Marsh Edge Trail will be closed during eagle nesting season since the nest is near the parking lot. During my several trips, the trail was open but the lookout tower was closed.

This .3-mile loop heads from the tree-covered parking area through a loblolly pine stand, the smell of which reminds me of Christmas time. A short boardwalk section and viewing platform is at the loop's apex. Take note of the three oval images—erosion is a problem all along the bay's marshland ecosystem. Just beyond is a bench with access to the marsh edge. At low tide, rich black soil is exposed and if you take one or two paces into what appears to be firm ground, you'll sink right to your boot tops . . . not that this has ever happened to me. The soil's texture is very odd—it's not quite rubbery, and not really firm either. Actually, it reminds me of the line from *Blazing Saddles*

Blackwater near the Marsh Edge Trail. As I was exiting the parking area, I spotted this eagle hanging out in a tree. Positioned at the limit of my 400mm lens I had to wait for the eagle to turn its head to pick up the morning sun. *Canon EOS 5D Mkii, Tamron 200-400, ISO200 setting, f8 @ 1/400s*

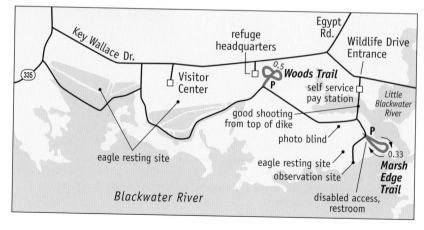

where Cleavon Little asks, "Charley, what ain't exactly water and ain't exactly earth?"

Finish the loop and head out along Wildlife Drive.

Hike 12 Lore of the Land Trail, Tuckahoe State Park, Caroline County

Type: walk	**Distance:** 0.85 miles
Rating: 3	**Time:** 1 hour
GPS: 38° 58.866'N 76° 55.943'W	**Elevation change:** 50 feet
Best time: any time	**Best lenses:** 20mm to 200mm
Difficulty: easy	

Directions: From the intersection of MD-313 and MD-311/287 in Goldsboro, take MD-313 (Goldsboro Road) west for 3.7 miles and turn left onto MD-312 south (South Oakland Road). In 3.4 miles turn right onto Cherry Lane. In 4.6 miles turn right into the state park camping entrance, follow the lane for another .2 miles, and bear right to park on the left in another .2 miles opposite the disc golf parking area. GPS coordinates: 38° 58.866'N, 76° 55.943'W.

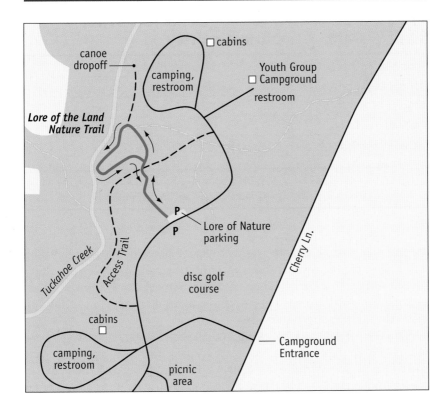

Pick up a brochure and head out along the yellow-blazed trail. As soon as you start out, bear left at a Y, then right about 30 yards later at a T. Left heads for the "campfire ring." You'll come to another trail crossing at .11 miles—go left and follow the arrow, then repeat the process again at .17 miles. The trail has a tendency to meander back on itself, so just follow the ample signs. At "Stop 7," notice the large tree that's down next to the trail. Next, at "Stop 9," you arrive at the remains of a National Champion tree—an overcup oak, a species of oak I'd never hear of. This one had a circumference of 21 feet 5 inches, was 118 feet tall, and had a massive crown spread of 120 feet. It went down many years ago, so all that's visible now is the hulk's well-decayed trunk.

I first hiked this trail in mid-November, well after peak color season. I enjoy trails with fresh, crunchy leaves—shorter trails, that is. Many hours of leaf crunching can get on the nerves. Regardless, as you wander along, find the occasional rock or log to sit on. My sunset sojourn was filled with crickets, tree frogs, and the sharp call of a nearby barred owl that came and went with the gentle breeze.

Hike 13 Tuckahoe Valley Trail and Pee Wee's Trail, Tuckahoe State Park, Caroline County

Type: hike	Distance: 5 miles
Rating: 4	Time: 2 hours
GPS: 38° 57.984′N 75° 56.448′W	Elevation change: 70 feet
Best time: any time	Best lenses: 20mm to 200mm
Difficulty: moderate	

Directions: See page 41. After turning right onto Cherry Lane, go 5.4 miles and turn right onto Crouse Mill Road, following signs for Tuckahoe Lake. Park on the left in a gravel parking area. GPS coordinates: 38° 57.984′N, 75° 56.448′W.

My first trip to Tuckahoe was as a small child with grandparents who had a church covered-dish supper at the small lake. More than forty years later here I am again, but on a frosty November dawn with low clouds glowing blood red overhead before fading to a softer rosy glow as the sun kisses the horizon through the trees.

From the parking area, go left up a small slope, keeping the lake on your left, then head right onto the blue-blazed Valley Trail at the sign kiosk. Soft soil with a slight give makes for comfortable walking and quiet footfalls. In the wee hours of morning, the softly lit trail invites you to venture deeper and deeper. At .52 miles the Piney Branch Trail merges from the left. In 20

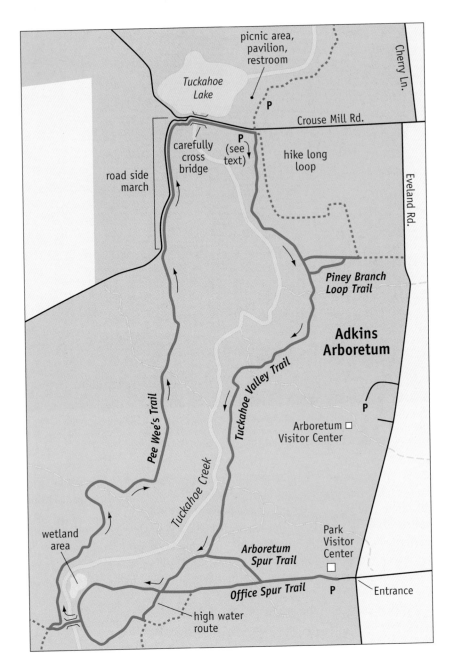

yards go right away from the Piney Branch Trail. Cross into the wonderful Adkins Arboretum property at .57 miles and make the first right. If you go left, you'll be on their trail network.

During the first half mile, a group of middle-aged African American men were running their hounds after squirrels. It has been a long time since I've seen this done, and I watched as the owners called and whistled to their

Tuckahoe Loop. This handheld shot was one of many I shot of the trail about .5-mile from the start. I settled on this little curve because it provided a nice leading arc through the scene. *Canon EOS 5D Mkii, Canon 20-105L, polarizer, ISO400 setting, f8 @ 1/30s*

dogs. In speaking to them, I learned that they used four types of whistle commands, like voice training, to send them in different directions. I did take note that the whistle for "come here" didn't seem to work, but as was stated to me, "It beats raking leaves." There's quite a dog culture on the eastern shore. Inland it's hounds and tracking dogs, and on the water it's retrievers and water dogs of all kinds. During hunting season, it seems like every pick-up has a dog or two in the back, and they couldn't be happier than when they're chasing something.

At .79 miles T into the arboretum's Upland Walk, turn right, and descend to cross a footbridge. At .91 miles bear right onto the Tuckahoe Creek Side Walk and then, after several whip-saw turns, come to a swampy area at 1.14 miles. Look around carefully, as this is excellent wildflower habitat. If you can get here in fog, you'll have perfect landscape conditions. When you get to the next T at 1.2 miles, turn right to pick up the south Tuckahoe Valley Trail. Pass by the Arboretum Spur Cutoff at 1.61 miles and T into the Office Spur Trail as you cross off the Adkins property at 1.8 miles. Turn right following the square blue blazes of the high-water route (not the blue triangles).

Arrive at a steel footbridge over Tuckahoe Creek at 2.16 miles, cross it, and turn right to follow Pee Wee's Trail, which is blazed orange. The trail climbs slowly as the Tuckahoe meanders away. After a long right turn, enter a farm field at 2.5 miles, continue moving right, and quickly re-enter the woods. The trail descends slightly only to climb again. Next, it swings left, only to go right again a short time later. It's well blazed, so feel free to set a brisk pace, or better yet make it a trail run. Cross another footbridge, a small one that crosses a quiet backwater tributary, at 2.86 miles. Have a seat here and let the woods speak to you.

After a long, quiet section of sandy trail, arrive at a Y at 3.75 miles and bear right at a sign (its white back is to you). Once you hit the road at 3.8 miles, you're in for a boring march back to your car. There's no pedestrian lane along the road and the grassy shoulder is slow-going, so move quickly and walk on the left toward oncoming traffic. When you get to the intersection near the lake, turn right and wait for a break in traffic before crossing the bridge in front of the dam. Again, there's no pedestrian lane, so take care and be quick! Arrive at your car at 5 miles.

If you have time, I encourage you to head over to the Adkins Arboretum, which is 1.2 miles south of Crouse Mill on Eveland Road. They have a wonderful property filled with local plants and trees. You can find them at www.adkinsarboretum.org.

Hike 14 Black Walnut Point Natural Resources Management Area, Talbot County

Type: walk	Distance: .67 miles
Rating: 3	Time: 15 minutes
GPS: 38° 40.640'N, 76° 20.617'W	Elevation change: none
Best time: sunset and early morning	Best lenses: 20mm to 200mm
Difficulty: easy	

Directions: Black Walnut Point is located at the southern tip of Tilghman Island, where MD-33 ends. From the intersection of MD-33 and MD-332 west of Easton, take MD-33 west away from Easton, following signs for Tilghman Island for 24.5 miles. You can park near the Coast Guard radio station or at a wide spot on the right past the gate adjacent to the trailhead. The road beyond the trailhead is the private access lane to the Black Walnut Point Inn. GPS coordinates: 38° 40.640'N, 76° 20.617'W.

This short loop through a very tight pine forest is a wonderful birding opportunity. Head up the woodchip-covered, red-blazed trail, and at .18 miles come to a Y at the loop trail's head. Turn right, and then immediately

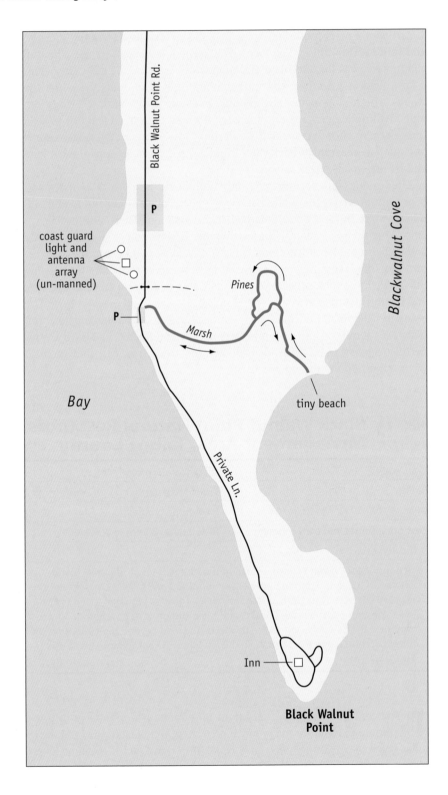

Black Walnut Point Rd.

P

coast guard
light and
antenna
array
(un-manned)

Pines

P

Marsh

Blackwalnut Cove

Bay

tiny beach

Private Ln.

Inn

**Black Walnut
Point**

turn right again at a T. At .27 miles, you get dumped out at a small beach filled with drift logs. You can carefully work your way to the right at low tide to get a view of Black Walnut Cove. Return to the T and head straight and make a quick loop, meeting up with the main access trail at .5 miles, and then get back to your car at .67 miles.

The narrow trail through the pines was kind of boring until I stopped to jot some notes. I dropped my journal, knelt down to retrieve it, and the woods came alive with dozens of little songbirds. I'm not very good at identifying birds without a field guide, which I didn't have. So I sat down and just watched. It had been breezy the entire day, but here in the late afternoon the weather had turned rough. I assumed that these little birds found the dense woods to be a nice sheltered location. As a light rain began to fall, I simply stayed still, moving only my head and eyes. At one point, a dozen birds were within a foot of my face, flitting between branches. A leg cramp ended our little moment of company together, and I walked back to my car with a broad smile. Waves were hitting the sheet pile bulkhead next it, and my car was crusty with salt. I didn't dare pull out my camera to photograph the sun as it dipped below a leaden sky. Yes, it's a short trail but, if you're patient, you may experience the kind of magic I did.

Hike 15 Terrapin Nature Park, Queen Anne's County

Type: walk	**Distance:** 3.25 miles
Rating: 4+	**Time:** 1 hour, 20 minutes
GPS: 38° 59.399'N, 76° 19.299'W	**Elevation change:** 20 feet
Best time: sunrise through midmorning and late afternoon	**Best lenses:** 20mm to 600mm
Difficulty: easy	

Directions: From US-301/50 exit 24 in Annapolis, take US-50 east across the Bay Bridge onto Kent Island, a total distance of 12.1 miles, and exit onto MD-8/Business Parkway northbound. In .4 miles turn left onto Skipjack Parkway; you'll be heading for a large water tower in the distance. In another .2 miles go left at a T onto Log Canoe Circle and enter a corporate park. In .4 miles turn left onto a somewhat hidden access and follow the lane to where it ends at a large paved parking area with a sign for Terrapin Nature Park. You might also see signage for The Cross Island Trail. GPS coordinates: 38° 59.399'N, 76° 19.299'W.

This 276-acre preserve feels much bigger than it is. The trails are flat, the paths are wide, the fields are filled with various flowers in the spring, the birds are accommodating, and the foxes are tolerant of big lenses. A small beach along the bay is also delightful, and two tidal pools harbor a variety of waterfowl. The 3.25-mile trail wanders through forest and field, and is popular among dog walkers and runners as well. The park is open dawn to dusk and there's a handicap-accessible trail leading to a nice gazebo.

Walk the paved path marked as the Cross Island Trail for a few dozen yards and bear left off of it, heading for a low-slung viewing platform. This is Meadow View. Return to the unpaved loop trail and turn right to head away from the paved Cross Island Trail. At .27 miles arrive at a T and continue straight ahead. In a few paces, come to a bird blind overlooking a tidal pool; bypass this since the marsh has overgrown the blind and there is no longer a view.

The gravel trail continues and crosses a dike that divides a north-reaching finger of the pool from the main body of water. There's a good view from here and I saw several kinds of ducks, most of whom were camera shy. They tended to stick to the pool edges where forage was much easier, and on the windy day I was here they stuck to areas sheltered from the stiff easterly wind. At .53 miles arrive at the gazebo overlooking the bay and the Preston Lane Jr. Memorial Bridge, aka US-50. There are many paths leading to the water's edge that afford good shooting positions. The major issue is the number of white-sided buildings along the shore and across the bay; be very careful about how you compose your shot to minimize their impact. Sunset silhouettes would probably work best.

As you move south with the bay on your right, you'll see an open marsh on the left. This is the marshy upland section of the tidal pool you crossed earlier and the best waterfowl shooting opportunity you'll have; you'll need your biggest lens. My 400mm lens, when attached to my Canon Rebel, has an effective focal length of 660mm, which is adequate. There are a couple of game trails through the brush but I'm not fond of going off the trail to press

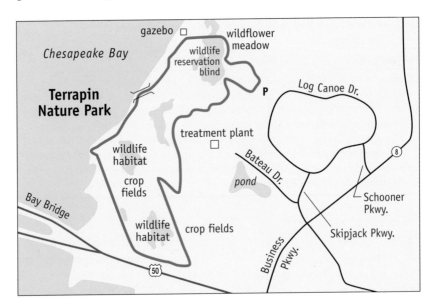

a wildlife photo. Whenever shooting critters, keep a keen eye on their behavior; if the animal's behavior changes, you've pushed too close too quickly. When it comes to little trails into the marsh here, or anywhere, use your best judgment and take it very, very slowly.

At .86 miles you'll cross a little footbridge where the marsh drains into the bay. Walk along another beach for a short distance, and at 1.05 miles come to a Y that heads to the 1.2-mile South Meadow Loop. Left returns to the parking area; go right to complete the loop, which runs along US-50.

As I walked slowly through a mowed field, jotting notes, I caught a glimpse of movement to my left. Taking a knee, I watched three nearly mature fox kits hunting voles or mice. They would move along with their heads up and ears tilted forward, only to suddenly stop, scan intently, then sprint a couple of feet and raise their heads, chomping down on a late breakfast. The entire time, one fox would watch me while the others hunted, each taking its turn as lookout. This went on for many minutes until the three paused, looked at each other as if voting on a decision, and wandered off to a more private hunting opportunity.

By now, you've probably noticed the trail has become an old farm lane that makes a long, slow left to come parallel to US-50 around 1.7 miles. At 1.81 miles make a hard left onto an old paved road, heading north away from US-50. Pass several mowed pathways leading into the meadow and surrounding fields. You'll find a manhole at 2.03 miles on the left and a closed road on the right that leads to a sewage plant. Ignore the two mowed paths that head left through the rushes. Continue straight in a northerly direction along the road. When you get to 2.3 miles, make a hard right onto a wide footpath as the road you were on connects with the northern end of the South Meadow Loop. The path loops back on itself as it avoids a tidal marsh and skirts the sewage plant. At 2.89 miles come to a T and turn right to head back to the parking area, arriving in 3.25 miles.

Hike 16 Headquarters Loop, Eastern Neck National Wildlife Refuge, Kent County

Type: walk	Distance: .25 miles
Rating: 3	Time: 10 minutes
GPS: 39° 1.316′N, 76° 13.794′W	Elevation change: 30 feet
Best time: early morning through late afternoon	Best lenses: 20mm to 400mm
Difficulty: easy	

Directions: Eastern Neck NWR is an island at the end of MD-445. From the intersection of MD-291 (Morgnec Road) and MD-20 (High Street) on the west side of Chestertown, take MD-20 west for 12.1 miles to the village of Rock Hall and turn left onto MD-445 south. In 8.2 miles turn right into the visitor center at Eastern Neck NWR. GPS coordinates: 39° 1.316′N, 76° 13.794′W.

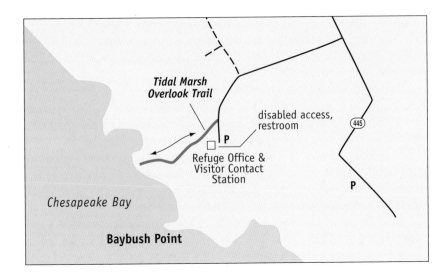

The access gate is automatic and opens at 7:30 A.M.; it closes one hour after sunset. Be sure to be on your way off the property before the sun hits the horizon. If you want to shoot in late light, you can do so at the island's north end near the Tubby Cove boardwalk (south of the Narrows Bridge). Also, there are fall and winter road/trail closures for bald eagle nesting season, so be flexible.

This short, handicap-accessible loop from behind the visitor center will wet your whistle, so to speak. The short trail takes you down a smooth path to a bird blind overlooking an osprey nesting platform. Nesting season is in the spring, so when I was here in the fall the nest wasn't active. A 400mm lens would be the minimum you'd need to shoot from the blind, but bring tele-extenders or a longer lens if you have them. Since the platform is above you, the birds will be viewed against the sky. If it's overcast any shot will be drab, so you need a day with a cobalt blue sky. Two wooden poles rising above the platform are problematic at best, and although I'm not a big fan of "photoshopping" out ungainly stuff in an image, this is a place where I'd say it's OK.

Hike 17 Wildlife Loop, Eastern Neck National Wildlife Refuge, Kent County

Type: walk	**Distance:** .5 miles
Rating: 3	**Time:** 30 minutes
GPS: 39° 1.851'N, 76° 13.466'W	**Elevation change:** 80 feet
Best time: early morning through late afternoon	**Best lenses:** 20mm to 400mm
Difficulty: easy	

Directions: See page 49. Continue on MD-445 south for 7.7 miles and park on the left in the signed lot for the Wildlife Loop. GPS coordinates: 39° 1.851'N, 76° 13.466'W.

See page 50 for gate information.

This very delightful woodland hike makes a .5-mile loop through a second-growth upland forest of mixed hardwoods. From the parking area, head right past the sign and take your time as you wander along. About halfway around the loop is a large oak that was hit by lightning. Large scorch marks on the surface and deep interior burns testify to lightning's power. The tree blew apart in two pieces about 15 feet up, and the crown dropped vertically to the ground. Continue around the loop and exit back into the lot well away from the sign you passed at the beginning.

Now drive north .4 miles and turn right onto Bogles Wharf Road. Follow it to the end, parking anywhere in the large lot, but not near the boat ramp or piers. The two docks and bulkhead make for the perfect spot to shoot Hail Cove and Durdin Creek inlet. The piers extend far enough into the small cove to get nice fall color shots of the trees opposite. The view extends from 80° left to 280° right, so morning light will work best for shooting.

Wildlife Loop at Eastern Neck. My time at Eastern Neck was filled with clouds and I was really looking for a nice image when I walked past this massive white oak, stopped, and gave it a big hug. This was the largest specimen I had seen in a couple days. *Canon EOS 5D Mkii, Canon 20-105L, polarizer, ISO100 setting, f8 @ 1/25s*

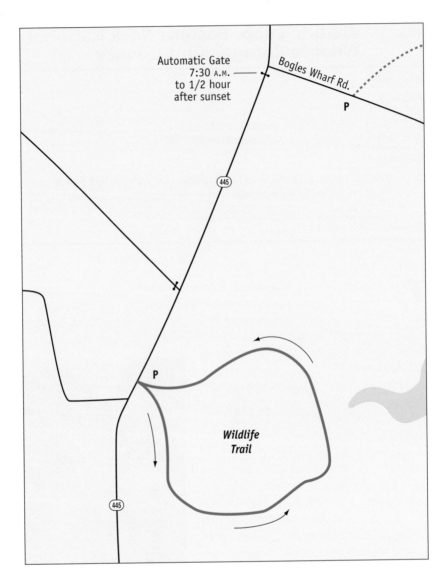

Automatic Gate
7:30 A.M.
to 1/2 hour
after sunset

Bogles Wharf Rd.

P

445

P

*Wildlife
Trail*

445

A sign shows an aerial image of how much the shoreline of Hail Cove has eroded in the past thirty or so years. This image is typical of all the marshes along the Chesapeake Bay, and the erosion is especially apparent at Blackwater NWR and Fishing Bay WMA. As the global sea level rises over the next few decades, even if it's only inches, a way of life will slowly be swallowed as the marshes of the Chesapeake dissolve into oblivion. It is places like this that bring a poignant reminder of the dangers of climate change. You don't need to look to faraway lands or Pacific Islands to see the effects; here it's right at your feet and before your eyes.

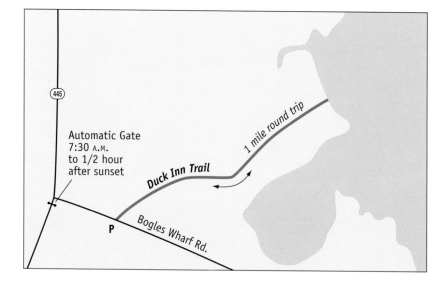

Hike 18 Duck Inn Trail, Eastern Neck National Wildlife Refuge, Kent County

Type: walk	**Distance:** 1 mile
Rating: 4+	**Time:** 45 minutes
GPS: 39° 2.178′N, 76° 13.191′W	**Elevation change:** 30 feet
Best time: early morning through late afternoon	**Best lenses:** 20mm to 400mm
Difficulty: easy	

Directions: See page 49. Continue on MD-445 south for 7.3 miles, then turn left onto Bogles Wharf Road. In about .1 miles, park on the right in the signed pull-out for the Duck Inn Trail. GPS Coordinates: 39° 2.178′N, 76° 13.191′W.

See page 50 for gate information.

Not many people use this trail, or at least not when I was here, so you should be able to enjoy some extreme quiet. Cross the road and head down the wide, grassy road, which follows a relatively dry high spot through the lowland marsh. At .3 miles a large opening facing north appears on the left. Taking a few steps off the trail will eliminate any foreground issues. You're a long way from any wildlife, so this is more of a landscape position; it's also an ideal sunrise location north of the refuge gate. Wander slowly through the marshes and after a subtle rise enter some pines near .35 miles. Pass the spot where the old inn once stood then, before you know it, come to the land's end at .5 miles. A small beach invites you to linger as you face the Chestertown River. The nearest spit of land on the left is Belts Bar

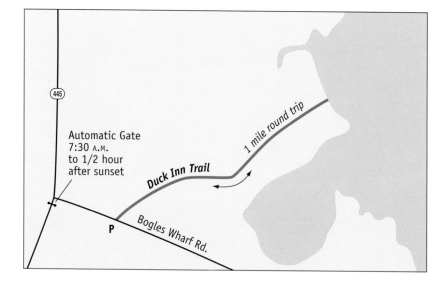

Point on the island's north end, and to the right is a small point guarding the entrance to Bogle Cove. The far shore is the northwest flank of Tilghman Island. If you head right or left to the beach edges, you'll find mounds large enough to stand on that place the rising sun behind you for landscape work. Drift logs lining the beach and shore make for interesting graphic designs, so bring your subtle artistic vision. Reverse your route to head back to your car.

Hike 19 Bayview-Butterfly Trail, Eastern Neck National Wildlife Refuge, Kent County

Type: walk	**Distance:** .25 miles
Rating: 3	**Time:** 10 minutes
GPS: 39° 1.939'N, 76° 14.387'W	**Elevation change:** 30 feet
Best time: early morning through late afternoon	**Best lenses:** 20mm to 400mm
Difficulty: easy	

Directions: See page 49. Continue on MD-445 south for 7.8 miles, then turn right onto Headquarters Road and follow it for 1 mile to the end. Park in the large gravel lot next to the Cape Chester House. GPS Coordinates: 39° 1.939'N, 76° 14.387'W.

See page 50 for gate information.

This short loop through a butterfly garden and grassy area sits atop a bluff overlooking the main channel of the Chesapeake Bay. Unlike refuges to the south, Eastern Neck is essentially a huge sand dune. As such, it affords

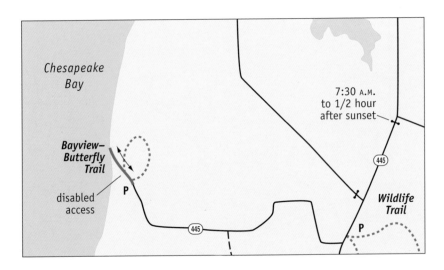

nice views such as this one, and supports a wide variety of tree species not seen in the marshland refuges below Kent Island.

Wander to your left, following the gravel path, and stop at the view platform. To your left, the four massive towers of the US-50 Chesapeake Bay Bridge dominate the view. Directly ahead, you can see the extreme northern end of Kent Island at Love Point. Looking more to the right, you can see steam plumes (in cooler weather) and two large towers on the horizon. This is a power plant near Baltimore. With a good set of binoculars, you'll be able to make out Sparrows Point.

Now take some time to complete the .25-mile loop around the field.

Hike 20 Tubby Cove Boardwalk and Boxes Point Trail, Eastern Neck National Wildlife Refuge, Kent County

Type: walk	Distance: 2 miles
Rating: 4	Time: 1 hour, 30 minutes
GPS: 39° 2.687'N, 76° 13.315'W	Elevation change: 30 feet
Best time: sunrise through sunset	Best lenses: 20mm to 400mm
Difficulty: easy	

Directions: See page 49. Continue on MD-445 south for 6.7 miles and park on the right in the large parking area at the Tubby Cove Boardwalk (the first parking area south of the Narrows Bridge). GPS Coordinates: 39° 2.687'N, 76° 13.315'W.

See page 50 for gate information.

Begin by heading out along the boardwalk to the first of two shooting locations—one is a tall platform and the other is an enclosed blind. The open tower has a good northeasterly exposure with a view from about 240° to 40°. You'll need a big lens, such as a 500mm or longer, or even tele-extenders, to shoot individual birds from either spot. As a scenic location, shooting from the boardwalk facing to the left (generally southwest) is best. Don't forget the classic shot straight down the boardwalk, either.

Head back to the parking area and turn left, walking up the road to the Tubby Cove trail on the right, about 150 yards up the road. The trail passes through a successional forest of loblolly pines as it follows the only dry ground between Boxes Point to the north and Belts Bar Point to the south. I heard and saw a pair of red-bellied woodpeckers and numerous red-winged black birds as I moved into the woods, so I simply sat down, as you should now, and let the birds calm down and adjust to my presence. After a few

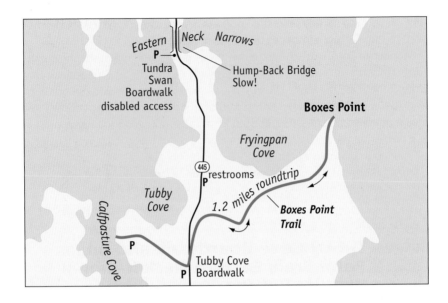

minutes, the woods came back to life with the noise of hundreds of birds going about their daily business. I'm no expert birder and I can identify only a few birds by ear, but I heard a couple dozen different species over the course of an hour as I slowly moved down the trail.

At .55 miles a pool becomes visible on the left, with a roughly southeast view into it. As I jotted this note, a bald eagle swooped low over the trail, moving casually toward the pond. A downy woodpecker plied its trade of insect hunting a few feet to my right, and half a dozen different nuthatches ladder-jacked their way up and down tall tree trunks in their entertaining tuxedo-clad inverted hop. A soft wind plied the pine needles with its calming and inviting sound, which is heard many seconds before it is felt. All the while, dozens of little birds flitted from branch to branch chattering away. I must say, this is a glorious way to spend an hour in the woods.

The trail's end brings you to an inviting bench near a little beach with a view spanning 20° to 150°. A short, weedy path left takes to you a marsh pond looking northwest. The boat pullout is part of an extensive bay-centric water trail system, and you can even circumnavigate Eastern Neck if you'd like. The opposite shore has no buildings or towers in view, making this a good sunrise spot.

When you've soaked up the view, reverse your route. When you hit the paved road turn left again, keeping left and facing traffic, and walk the 150 yards back to your car at the Tubby Cove Boardwalk.

Hike 21 **Turkey Point Lighthouse, Elk Neck State Park, Cecil County**

Turkey Point

Type: cliff	**Height:** 95 feet
Rating: 5+	**Best time:** late afternoon through sunset
GPS, parking: 39° 27.490′N, 76° 0.474′W	**Difficulty:** easy
GPS, vista: 39° 26.983′N, 76° 0.501′W	**Distance:** 1.6 miles
Faces: 189°	**Time:** 45 minutes
Field of view: 114° to 264°	**Elevation change:** 100 feet
Relief: 95 feet	**Best lenses:** 17mm to 200mm
Elevation difference: 95 feet	

Directions: From the I-95 exit 100 south of Elkton and Newark, Delaware, take MD-272 south for 13.8 miles. Pass the ranger station and park in front of a gate where the pavement ends at a large parking lot. GPS coordinates: 39° 27.490′N, 76° 0.474′W.

This easy road hike has one grade, and it's the opening 50-plus yards. After winding through trees and crossing a large field, the trail ends at a tiny lighthouse. Perched well back from the bluffs overlooking the Chesapeake's

Turkey Point Lighthouse. As you can see, Turkey Point Lighthouse is quite small. I settled on a twilight shot, trying to get the white tower to pick up the pastel sky glow. Moving a little left and right allowed me to find a nice position for the background tree. *Canon EOS 5D Mkii, Canon 20-105L, polarizer, ISO100 setting, f16 @ 13s*

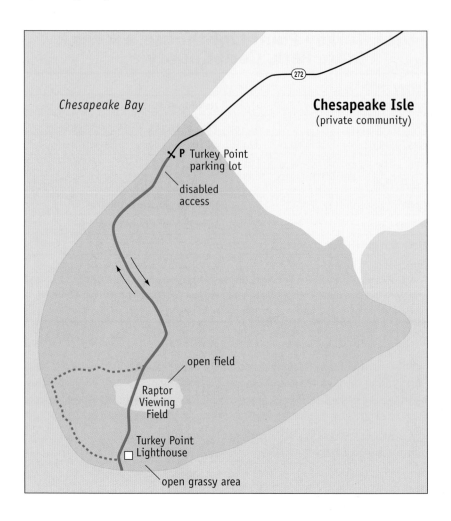

headwaters, the view is impressive but not as wide as one would expect. The light was only meant to be seen from a southerly direction, so the surrounding forest is not cut back as far it might have been. Wander to the sidewalk's end and carefully look down. Believe it or not, you're only 95 feet above the bay, although it feels much higher. The view east takes in the hamlet of Crystal Beach, and the view to the west is nothing but open water. You can't really see northwest toward the Susquehanna River, but when the light is right you can make out a southerly current passing the point.

I like shooting the lighthouse during twilight. Impressive as the view is, the blank bay surface is unappealing unless you're working with spectacular atmospherics. The technique to shooting the light is what I call "walking the clock." Start with a "normal" focal length of 50mm to 70mm, pick any spot and call it "noon," then shoot a few frames, placing the light in different frame positions. Now move to 1 o'clock, then 2 o'clock, and so on until you've circled the light. Change focal lengths and get far away, then walk right up to it. At some point, your most pleasing composition will reveal itself. Repeat the whole process again as the light changes and the stars come out. Not a bad way to end the day, is it?

Hike 22 Beaver Marsh Trail, Elk Neck State Park, Cecil County

Type: hike	**Distance:** 2.0 miles
Rating: 5	**Time:** 50 minutes
GPS: 39° 28.079'N 75° 59.172'W	**Elevation change:** 230 feet
Best time: any time	**Best lenses:** 17mm to 200mm
Difficulty: moderate	

Directions: From I-95 exit 100 south of Elkton and Newark, Delaware, take MD-272 south for 12.4 miles and turn left onto Rogues Harbor Road. In .5 miles bear left into the large boat trailer parking area and park near the lot's north end, away from the boat ramp. GPS coordinates: 39° 28.079'N, 75° 59.172'W.

Check the local tide charts before you begin. The opening move in this hike is to cross a beach about 70 yards long that can be completely covered (but not impassable) at high tide. Tide tables can be found on the National Oceanic and Atmospheric Administration website at http://tidesandcurrents.noaa.gov/tide_predictions.shtml. Select "Maryland," then "Town Point Wharf" under "Elk River." You can get tables in a variety of formats that can be easily downloaded onto a smartphone.

This 2-mile loop of Beaver Marsh climbs and descends a number of times, is well-

Beaver Marsh Loop. The cloudy weather made the marsh unphotogenic, but the same weather made the low ground cover glow in a wonderful muted light. This handheld shot was one of several dozen. I'd shoot a couple frames, then move a couple feet and shoot again. This is near the loop's north end. Canon EOS 5D Mkii, Canon 20-105L, polarizer, ISO100 setting, f8 @ 1/13s

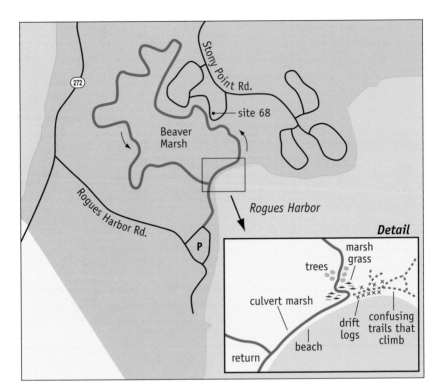

signed and blazed, and makes a nice starter hike for kids who are old enough to handle climbs and descents of 60 feet or so.

From the parking area, head down the wide, yellow-blazed gravel path, passing the large sign and keeping the bay on your right. After passing the 3-mile long White Cliffs trail, arrive at the marsh at .2 miles. Stand on the large casement of rocks with the beach ahead and your return route on the left. Cross the beach to the casing rocks on the far side of the marsh and turn so that your back is to the bay. Stop and look around at the numerous footpaths that braid this area. The marsh is to your left, an obvious footpath climbs uphill to the right, and the beach continues on farther to the right. Any trail that climbs up to the right is the wrong trail.

A number of drift logs will be near the marsh edge, driven slightly inland along the base of the little hill. The red-blazed trail heads hard left between the marsh and the hill and past the logs on your right, remaining at beach level. You'll be almost parallel to the beach as you pass through some bulrushes and over some muddy soil, only to swing right after about 20 yards. There will be several unmarked paths for the next few dozen yards—no matter what, follow the red blazes carefully.

After a short climb, pop out into the campground at .5 miles near site #68. Continue a few more paces, then go left off the road. The trail falls and then climbs as it skirts the Wye Loop of the campground on the right. The surface will be comfortable sandy soil with occasional heavy forest cover. At .95 miles go past the yellow connector to Stony Point Road. Also bypass the next one to the White Cliffs trail at 1.15 miles.

In the next .2 miles, the trail drops to near marsh level, only to climb again for less height now at 1.4 miles. Pause here for a moment. From this grassy woodland, you can make some interesting woodland scenes of old, textured logs nestled in the lovely green grass. Continue ahead and drop again, finally coming to marsh level on its southwest side. Two view cutouts are quite nice, but unfortunately there weren't any wading birds around to shoot when I was there.

At 1.6 miles swing right way from the marsh to climb into the woods once again. The trail makes a looping meander to avoid a small drainage sluice and its associated habitat. After climbing about 50 feet, you're now at the head of the drainage sluice, where'll you make a hard left and run parallel to the way you came up, hitting the marsh again at 1.85 miles. Make your way back to the casement rocks where you started, turn your back to the marsh, and head back to your car on the gravel road, arriving at 2.05 miles.

Hike 23 White Clay Cliffs, Elk Neck State Park, Cecil County

White Clay Cliffs

Type: cliff	Height: 200 feet
Rating: 4	Best times: late afternoon through sunset
GPS, parking: 39° 29.244′N, 75° 59.535′W	Difficulty: easy
GPS, vista: 39° 29.016′N, 75° 59.704′W	Distance: .6 miles
Faces: 245°	Time: 35 minutes
Field of view: 220° to 270°	Elevation change: 100 feet
Relief: 200 feet	Best lenses: 17mm to 200mm
Elevation difference: 200 feet	

Directions: From I-95 exit 100 south of Elkton and Newark, Delaware, take MD-272 south for 11.3 miles, passing the ranger station, and turn right onto Mauldin Road. In .3 miles keep left and continue to climb the hill. Park in the large loop at the top. GPS coordinates: 39° 24.244′N, 75° 59.535W.

The route is well blazed and signed, and easy to follow except for one turn. The cliffs provide an incredible view of the bay, but it can be difficult to deal with the overhanging trees. All of the cliff edges are undercut, sometimes many feet back from the visible edge. A root network holds the soil together, and the softer sands and clays erode from below in a series of slumps. When it rains, water penetrates the upper few feet of clay, softening it to the point that it peels from the cliff face like plaster leaving soil mats hanging in space. They may look firm, but once you set foot on them you know you're in trouble because it feels like a firm trampoline. When shooting from any ledges at Elk Neck, stay back at least three feet, especially at the lighthouse because the amount of foot traffic it gets weakens the exposed edges.

Walk past the hilltop shelter, following the red blazes of the Mauldin Mountain Loop. (You'll also see some old white blazes here and there.) At .18 miles the trail starts a slow descent through handsome woods. Shortly after at .2 miles, come to a T where the red-blazed trail goes downhill to the right and also ahead. This is the head of a short loop. Go straight, and at .22 miles come to a signed Y where the red-blazed Mauldin Trail goes right and the yellow/green connector to White Banks goes left. Head left, and in another few yards come to another Y where red goes left and green/red goes right. Go right and uphill on the now-red White Banks Trail.

Come to a cliff at .3 miles with a narrow view through the trees, facing northwest at 39° 28.965′N, 75° 59.682′W. To the right, you can see the I-95 bridge over the Susquehanna River. Follow the red blazes downhill a short distance to another exposure that sits off a little side trail, just a few paces off the red blazes. This is the better view.

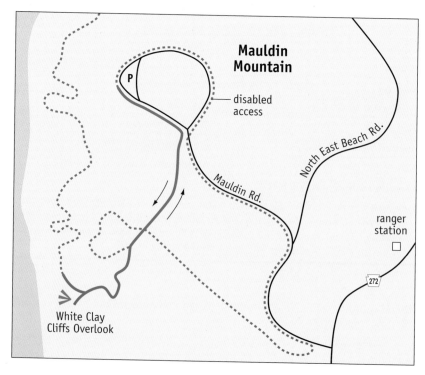

White Cliffs Overlook. A featureless bay and a featureless sky were just unworkable until this kayak geology tour wandered by. I doubt they saw me, but I could hear the entire lecture. *Canon EOS 5D Mkii, Canon 20-105L, polarizer, ISO100 setting, f4 @ 1/100s*

Framed by a couple small trees, this view is more southwest and easier to work. Set your tripod as low as possible, opening the legs out flat and shooting from ground level to keep overhanging limbs out of the frame if you can. Reverse your route and follow the signage back to the parking area.

As I got back to the parking area, I heard the distinctive scream of a bald eagle. A second later, a large female swooped through the trees a couple dozen yards away. This immature bird made no sound as its wings beat the air to gain altitude, moving away from me. I found this rather odd since during other close eagle encounters I've heard their wing beats as they claw at the air or the incredible whoosh as they glide by a few feet above my head. Why this bird was as silent as an owl I don't know, but it was one heck of a moment.

Hike 24 Fair Hill Natural Resources Management Area, Cecil County

Type: hike	Distance: 3.5 miles
Rating: 4+	Time: 1 hour, 20 minutes
GPS: 39° 42.620′N, 75° 50.293′W	Elevation change: 437 feet
Best time: any time	Best lenses: 17mm to 200mm
Difficulty: moderate	

Directions: From I-95 exit 100 for MD-272, take MD-272 north for 5.5 miles and turn right onto MD-273 east. In 6.0 miles turn left onto MD-213 and follow a tree-covered road that opens up into vast, open pasture land. In .3 miles turn right on Training Center Road and immediately bear left. Follow the gravel and macadam drive for 1.4 miles (you'll be heading north, then loop back south), and when you get to a T, turn right to stay on Training Center Road. In .4 miles turn left onto Tawes Drive, pass the visitor center, and after 1.1 miles park in the large dirt lot on the left near the covered bridge. GPS coordinates: 39° 42.620′N, 75° 50.293′W.

My wife was looking at my Maryland *Gazetteer* and noticed the name "Fair Hill"; she asked if I'd ever heard of it, to which I replied no. I was very pleasantly surprised. Fair Hill is quite well known in riding and equestrian circles, but not so much in hiking and biking. The 5,613-acre property, once part of the DuPont empire, has 75 miles of trails, a capacity of two hundred horse campers, two race tracks, and much more. There are five color-coded trails, ranging from 2.5 miles to 5.8 miles, which can be combined to create a longer outing. If you're a trail runner, this is the place to train, particularly if you're into ultra-marathons. You can easily create a series of loops totaling 12 miles with this parking area as the central supply

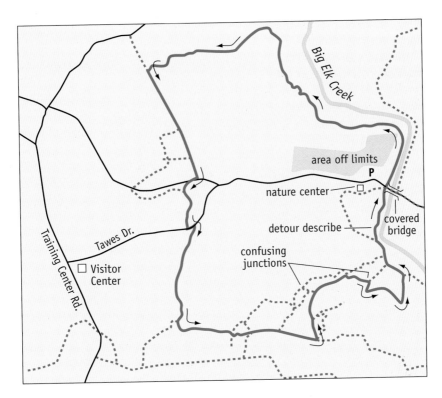

node. Fair Hill is the place to rattle off a nice 36-mile training run. Because there is so much, I'll concentrate on the 5.8-mile Orange loop.

From the large dirt parking area, face the bridge and go left (north), following a wide gravel lane adjacent to Big Elk Creek. As you approach a metal bridge, bear left and slightly uphill, cross the road, and continue uphill, following the orange blazes. The climb is comfortable but steady. Top out above Big Elk Creek at .37 miles. Look to your right for a footpath paved with native stone and make a brief descent to a rocky outcrop with a nice leaves-off view of the creek some 80 feet below. It's also a nice spot to listen to the birds.

For the next .3 miles the trail maintains a level line by meandering left and right. At .67 miles bear right at a Y to keep with the wider of two dirt paths. A short time later, go left at a + junction, now at .72 miles. Packed earth has given way to rock scree making for slower going. At .8 miles break out of the woods into a sun-filled field, only to re-enter the woods at .9 miles. Come to an intersection with a white blaze at 1.02 miles and cross it to stick with the orange blazes. Next is a Y at 1.24 miles, where orange goes right and left; note the signage—left is for horses, so go right to follow the road apple-free orange. The other orange trail rejoins at 1.35 miles. Cross a gravel road at 1.54 miles near Tawes Drive and again stick with the hiker's orange, immediately crossing a little creek. After a quick climb, hang a hard left at the edge of a field, now at 1.56 miles. The gravel road will be below and to the left.

Hit Tawes Drive at 1.74 miles, go left and then immediately go right onto a gravel road that skirts a field edge, then go right again quickly to re-enter the woods. You'll see a brown "Unsuitable for Equestrian Use" warning sign. At 1.96 miles, pop out at a field edge once again. This would be an incredible fall color spot with such a vast field surrounded by trees in peak color at dawn.

Arrive at a T at 2.04 miles; to the right is a .8-mile jaunt to Lot #1 (bow hunter parking on the map)—go left. Hit yet another T at 2.20 miles, go right, and then quickly go left. At 2.43 miles is a Y where a yellow-blazed "Park Quest" trail goes right while your orange-blazed trail goes left, then immediately left yet again in about 40 yards. Over the next 100 yards the trail descends, with numerous side trails branching in every direction—stick with the well-blazed orange.

Pass a nature trail at 2.8 miles, then go right. Another series of little jogs and intersections follows, and then at 3.8 miles arrive at a Y. Go left and descend; you'll see a little orange "A 28" sign. The trail descends, twisting as it goes through a quiet forest. Arrive at Big Elk Creek again at 3.25 miles. The trail swings left to run parallel to the creek on your right. At 3.30 miles, find some stairs (yellow Park Quest blaze) on your right and descend them to the creek. Here you'll find a shooting position for the bridge on a sandbar jutting into the creek. In front is a deep, sand-bottomed eddy that's easily chest-deep, so don't dump your gear into it. Follow a creek-side yellow blaze, the Park Quest Trail. Several little footpaths to the right lead to rocks that provide nice shooting perches; the best is a concrete slab 50-plus yards downstream of the bridge. There's a nice riffle created by it that smoothes the water flow, so the Tuscan red bridge will be reflected by water as smooth as glass—what a fall color shot this would make. Several pale or mud-covered rocks will have to be dampened to avoid highlights, or you can do some Photoshop work later, which you'll need anyway to get rid of the power line spanning the creek.

As I sat on a boulder jotting these notes, dozens of white butterflies gathered on the mud at my feet. There were a few yellow and orange ones as well. They just sat, their wings slowly flexing, as they sipped at the turbid water. Then a belted kingfisher shot below the bridge, heading downstream toward me, its characteristic jittery scream shattering the silence as it circled me, finally coming to rest in a tree above the large, fish-filled eddy. This was the highlight of the hike for me.

Head for the bridge and arrive back at your car at 3.5 miles.

If this little orange morsel wasn't enough for you, cross the bridge and add the 5.5-mile green loop and/or the 3.8-mile blue loop. If you're still not satisfied, tack on the 3.2-mile yellow loop for a nice 16-mile day.

Hike 25 Double Rock Falls, Double Rock Park, Baltimore County

Double Rock Falls

Type: Slide	**Difficulty:** easy
Rating: 2	**Distance:** .8 miles
GPS: 39° 22.212'N, 76° 31.619'W	**Time:** 30 minutes
Stream: Stemmers Run	**Elevation change:** 80 feet
Height: 8 feet	**Best lenses:** 20mm to 70mm

Directions: From exit 32 on the I-695 for US-1 (the Baltimore beltway on the north-east side), take US-1 north a short distance to Rossville Road and turn left. Follow Rossville Road northwest for .8 miles (when you cross Walther Boulevard at .5 miles, Rossville Road becomes Putty Hill). As soon as you cross over the beltway, turn left onto Fowler Avenue. In .5 miles turn right onto Hiss Avenue, then go left in .2 miles on Glen Road (a school is ahead on the right). In just under .2 miles, when you come even with Texas Avenue, turn left into the park and find a shady spot to park. GPS coordinates: 39° 22.337'N, 76° 31.670'W.

D ouble Rock Falls is popular with event photographers, and I saw two here shooting family portraits for Easter. The picnic pavilions had small groups, and the large parking lots speak to how crowded it can get. However, when this seasonal stream gets a good soaking nobody but landscape shooters will be out, which is when you should be here—in bad weather.

Head out from the parking area on a blue-blazed trail that follows Stemmers Run on the left-hand side. At .41 miles arrive at the falls and cross above them to access the more picturesque right-hand side.

The fall is two parallel slides over an outcropping of gneiss. In John Means's book, *Roadside Geology of Maryland*, he describes the formation as "Cambrian intrusive gneiss, perhaps of the Baltimore Mafic Complex." It's a mouthful, simply saying this is really hard, really old rock called Perry

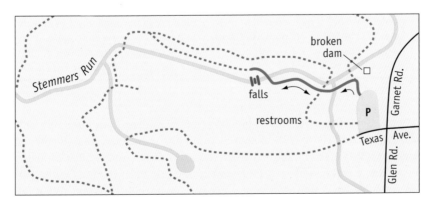

Hall Gneiss. This series of ledges defines what is called the "fall line," which separates the coastal plain to the south from the piedmont, ridge, and valley regions to the north and west. Think of somebody plowing a snow-covered parking lot. The lot isn't completely covered; instead, there are large patches separated by asphalt. Along comes the snow plow, sweeping the islands of snow against a wall to form a big mound. If you cut through the mound, you'll be able to identify the individual snow patches. Now, suppose the snow mound melts a little and then refreezes. The asphalt near it is covered in a sheen of ice—this is the coastal plain, and the edge of the mound is the fall line. In geologic language this is called *accretion*, and it's how the East Coast and the Appalachians were formed. Actually, it's more complicated than that, but you get the idea. Means's book is a great companion to have when exploring Maryland, and mine is quite dog-eared.

Reverse your route and head back to your car, arriving at .8 miles. And don't forget to bring your geology guide.

Hike 26 Hilton Area to Cascade Falls, Patapsco Valley State Park, Baltimore County

Cascade Falls

Type: slide	**Difficulty:** moderate
Rating: 3+	**Distance:** 3.9 miles
GPS: 39° 14.418'N, 76° 45.067'W	**Time:** 1 hour, 30 minutes
Stream: Cascade Run	**Elevation change:** 800 feet
Height: 9 feet	**Best lenses:** 20mm to 70mm

Directions: From I-95 near Baltimore, make your way to exit 47 on the city's southwest corner and follow signs for MD-166 north toward Catonsville, where you'll end up on I-195 west. As the expressway ends, exit onto MD-166 north (S. Rolling Road), and in 1.6 miles turn left onto Brook Road (you'll pass the entrance for the Community College of Baltimore). In .3 miles go left again, this time onto Hilton Avenue, and in 1.2 miles turn right into the Hilton Area parking loop. GPS coordinates: 39° 14.699'N, 76° 44.800'W. Admission is $3.00, and the gate opens at 8:00 A.M. For free parking or off-hours, begin at South Hilltop Road (Point of Interest 43 on the park map) at GPS coordinates: 39° 15.169'N, 76° 45.642'W.

Patapsco Valley State Park is big. It runs for 32 miles, from just south of I-295 all the way to MD-32 near Sykesville, and includes 16,043 acres of land and 170 miles of trails. Whether you're a casual flatland biker or jogger or walker, a serious hiker or trail runner, or a crazed ultra-marathoner, Patapsco Valley has a trail with your name on it just waiting for you. What fol-

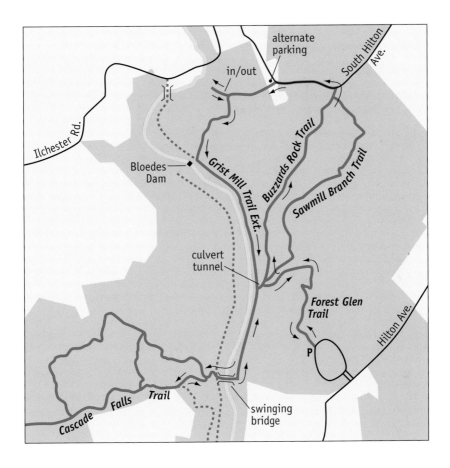

lows is just a small portion of this suburban wonder that has become a favorite of mine.

From the parking loop, make your way to the loop's northwest corner and locate the blue-blazed Forest Glen Trail. Follow it to the Patapsco River. The rocky, heavily used trail descends steeply to .3 miles, where it swings left to join a weakly flowing run. Follow the run, continuing downhill to a railroad culvert at .6 miles where the run sluices through a large tunnel. The tunnel will be your return route, so turn right and cross the little run to pick up the yellow-blazed Buzzards Rock Trail. In a few yards, come to a Y where the red-blazed Sawmill Trail goes right and the steep, rocky, deeply incised yellow-blazed trail goes straight. Head uphill on the yellow-blazed trail.

The climb ends when the heights are gained at .8 miles, after which you arrive at Buzzards Rock at .87 miles (Point of Interest 46 on the park map). A short side trail descends to several boulders, one of which has an upstream view of Bloedes Dam (Point of Interest 45 on the park map). It's an attractive long lens shot along 92° that would be especially nice in fall color.

Continue along the now-level yellow-blazed trail and cross a power line at 1.05 miles, where the trail surface becomes a gravel road. The red-blazed Sawmill Trail joins from the right at 1.3 miles near a paddock next to South Hilltop Road. Bear left to parallel the road and cross the power line again at a parking area on South Hilltop Road at 1.5 miles. Continue with the yellow-blazed Buzzards Rock Trail, while several un-blazed trails crisscross and diverge from your path.

At 1.7 miles come to a Y where the green-blazed Blackwater Rocks Trail pitches off the ridge to the right. Go right. This little loop drops and dumps you at a rock slab with a view of the valley. Head left around the viewpoint and rejoin the yellow-blazed trail at 1.71 miles. Here you'll find another Y— go right. A steep descent with lots of root-grabbing follows and lands you on the riverside bike trail (a paved road) at 2.1 miles. Go left and pass by the Bloedes Dam at 2.14 miles.

The level rail trail, called the Grist Mill Trail Extension, is filled with bikes, joggers, and a very large number of strollers. Everyone was keeping right and yielding appropriately. The rail trail runs close to the river and there are ample places to enter it and shoot. Between the dam and the swing bridge, I found at least twenty places to hop in. Return to the creek tunnel near the hike's start at 2.5 miles. Continue along the paved road to the swing bridge, which you'll cross at 2.8 miles.

Once on the river's far side, cross the heavily traveled road and climb the stairs near the parking area, then head left on a blue-blazed trail and arrive at the base of Cascade Falls at 3.1 miles. This pleasant fall is really a series of boulder chokes that create a complex sequence of chutes and burbles. The lowest is an attractive little funnel between two boulders, which makes for an intimate little landscape. A couple of dozen yards beyond the blue-blazed trail, the creek crosses at the true, 9-foot-tall Cascade Falls. Its lovely moss-covered drop with an attractive fan at its base and healthy forest cover above is a first-class location. Its plunge pool is formed by logs and its small size will require wide-angle work—take care with your depth of field. The creek above is filled with little rapids and chutes and you can work for up to .3 miles above the drop to the blue-blazed loop trail junction. On any nice day, this trail and the falls area will be mobbed, making shooting impossible. Get here early whenever the weather is bad and you'll have the place to yourself.

Reverse course and head back downhill to the swing bridge, cross, and go left, returning to the little tunnel at 3.6 miles. Go right, pass through the tunnel, and bear right on the blue-blazed Forest Glen Trail. Make the steep climb back out of the valley and arrive back at the parking loop near 3.9 miles. Now try to remember where you parked . . . yep, it happens to all of us.

Hike 27 Raven Rock Falls, Gunpowder Falls State Park, Baltimore County

Raven Rock Falls

Type: cascade over cascade	**Difficulty:** easy
Rating: 3	**Distance:** 2 miles
GPS: 39° 37.111'N, 76° 39.138'W	**Time:** 50 minutes
Stream: Raven Run	**Elevation change:** 100 feet
Height: 70 feet	**Best lenses:** 17mm to 70mm

Directions: From I-83 exit 27 north of Timonium, head east on MD-137 for Hereford. Take MD-137 east (Mt. Carmel Road) for .4 miles and turn left onto MD-45 north. Follow MD-45 for 1.4 miles. As you descend a hill toward the Falls Branch, there will be yellow caution signs ahead indicating the road swings left. Look for a large gravel parking area on the left between two telephone poles, within sight of the bridge over the run, and park on the left. GPS coordinates: 39° 36.806'N, 76° 39.549'W.

Hurry downhill along the road, cross the bridge and MD-45, hop the guardrail, and head downstream along Falls Branch's left-hand bank. You'll be on a blue-blazed trail that sidehills above the creek before dropping close beside it. After .78 miles come to a small stream that enters from the

left and tumbles over some rock and boulders before running over a wide rock face. This is Raven Rock Falls. Head uphill along Raven Run's right-hand side and work your way up approximately 70 feet to gain the cascade's head.

Raven Rock Falls is a seasonal series of small slides and drops tumbling over a shattered rock face. The lowest slide is the longest and least photogenic at low flow. About 20 yards above is an attractive little fan, and just above that a 5-foot cascade. Above this is an attractive sequence of little S-curves broken into 4- or 5-foot steps until the grade relaxes and the drops cease.

Raven Rock Falls. The falls are made of several smaller drops and this little cascade is about one third of the way up to the top. It was a tight space and required a very low setup, not easy to do with bifocals. *Canon EOS 5D Mkii, Canon 20-105L, polarizer, ISO100 setting, f14 @ 5s*

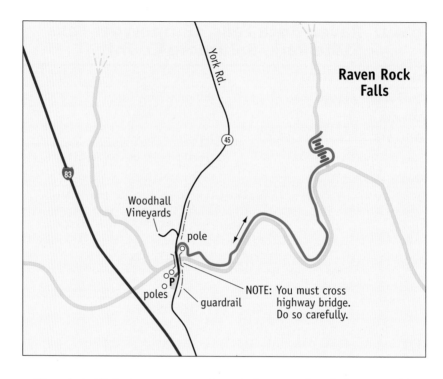

The whole 70-foot arrangement is an intimate series of shots, requiring tight, wide-angle work and maximum depth of field to look right. I also recommend macro gear since there are some lovely mosses and a good chance at some nice early wildflowers.

Hike 28 Sweet Air, Gunpowder Falls State Park, Harford County

Type: hike	**Distance:** 4.9 miles
Rating: 5	**Time:** 2 hours
GPS: 39° 32.172'N, 76° 30.313'W	**Elevation change:** 400 feet
Best time: any time	**Best lenses:** 20mm to 100mm
Difficulty: moderate	

Directions: From the US-1 bypass in Bel Air, take US-1 south and turn right onto MD-147 south (Harford Road). In 1.1 miles, turn right onto MD-152 north (Fallston Road) and follow it for 5.3 miles to MD-165 (Baldwin Mill Road) in the village of Upper Cross Roads. A strip-shopping center will be on the right and a gas station on the far corner. Take MD-165 south for just .3 miles and bear right onto Greene Road. Follow Greene Road for 1.2 miles and bear right onto Moores Road, then cross a creek and pass under power lines. In another .5 miles turn right onto Dalton-Bevard Road and look for a large gravel lot on the right in .2 miles. GPS coordinates: 39° 32.172'N, 76° 30.313'W.

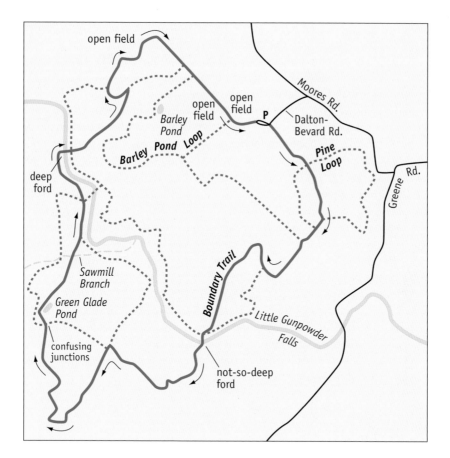

The boundary trail is a long loop around this little-known section of Gunpowder Falls State Park. This moderate, 4.9-mile loop crosses the Little Gunpowder River twice. On both occasions the river will overtop your boots, so bring old sneakers to change into. Photographically, the Little Gunpowder River is nice but the numerous swampy areas along the several side streams and seeps are better. These wet areas will support an array of wildflowers, which I missed out on. The route is well signed, and for trail runners it offers an ideal mix of terrain variation and navigation. I enjoyed my time immensely.

Begin by stopping at the sign kiosk to take some cell phone shots of the map. Head toward the woods, away from the kiosk, to the top end of the parking lot and turn right onto a mowed path to head away from the Barely Pond Loop. Follow the path along the parking lot downhill to Dalton Bevard Road, cross it, and climb up a pine tree-lined woods lane. Come to a T at .16 miles and go left; shortly after, bear left again to stay with the dirt trail. Next, cross the yellow-blazed Pine Log Trail at .31 miles. You'll T into the yellow-blazed trail at .44 miles. Head right on the signed, blue-blazed Boundary

Trail. Heading uphill, join the yellow-blazed trail at a field edge. At .53 miles go left at the signage with the birdhouse on top.

After passing some houses, bypass the white-blazed Little Gunpowder Trail at .76 miles and head straight into the woods ahead, passing between several trees with blue blazes. Exit the woods in short order and go left at a T that's a mowed path at .86 miles. After a brief climb, come to another birdhouse signpost at .96 miles. This rather confusing intersection has a lot happening. Take the hard left, following the blue blazes and passing a small brown sign with a poem on it. Descend a muddy path, crossing the white-blazed Gunpowder Trail at 1.11 miles. At the next sign go left toward the Little Gunpowder River, arriving at 1.2 miles. Look for a good spot to ford and try not to slip on the rocky bottom.

After crossing, bear right then immediately left to climb out of the river valley. Arrive at another T at 1.39 miles and go right, away from the High Rock Overlook. The trail climbs for the next .2 miles, sometimes steeply, meandering as it goes. Keep a sharp eye for blazes; as soon as you exit the woods into a field edge at 1.55 miles, go right on a dirt path. To the left is an old silo. A confusing set of blazes is painted on trees well off the trail to the right at 1.71 miles and they lead into sticker bushes. Continue ahead a short distance of about 35 yards along the field edge and, as the trail begins to sweep left, look for a well-trodden right turn away from the field. Go right, and in a few more yards you will see a metal "Emergency Vehicles Only" sign on the right.

Shortly after the emergency vehicles sign, go left at the bench/sign combination and descend slightly. Pass the orange-blazed Green Glade Trail at 1.85 miles. After descending a deeply incised old woods road, cross a muddy-bottomed stream at 2.02 miles and T into another woods road at a signed right turn. At 2.24 miles bear right at a Y, passing an old blowdown on the right. Make a slow descent and bear right at another Y at 2.38 miles, following an old, faded blue blaze.

The trail becomes rough for a bit, after which you pass an orange-blazed trail at 2.49 miles. Bear left at the next sign where the blue blazes are newer and easier to follow. Arrive at Green Glade Pond at 2.56 miles. I saw a fairly large snapping turtle here. Follow the muddy trail downhill to cross the Saw Mill Branch at 2.74 miles; you'll have an easier time on this ford than on the last one. When you get to the orange Saw Mill Branch sign just after crossing, swing left on the muddy path, then bear left at a signed Y to climb up a small slope away from the Gunpowder River. Now go right at a red crossing trail sign. This whole sequence happens between the creek crossing and 2.85 miles—essentially .1 miles of turns and signs.

At 2.93 miles go left. When you hit the gas line right-of-way at 3.13 miles, head right to cross the deep, slow-moving Gunpowder River. I took my boots off and did it barefoot, which was not comfortable on a bracingly cold April day. It only took a minute, but the chilly water made each rock more painful than the last as I approached the far bank. There's a tendency to rush the last several steps—resist, because a fall in this cold water would not be good with 2 miles to go. When I finally got across, my feet were pink and very sore. I didn't know how deep the ford would be so I didn't have old socks, sneakers, or water shoes to wear. Duh!

After crossing, head straight uphill, following the wide gas line. In 60 yards, go left at a signed double blaze and, after an easy climb, T into the white trail at 3.77 miles and go left following the blue signage. Shortly after, come to a well-signed Y and go right toward a field. Follow the field edge to 4.01 miles and head right into the woods, where a red dot trail goes straight at the signpost.

Houses will be on the left for the next .3 miles. At 4.18 miles, come to a signpost on the right where the trail leads right into the woods. Go straight along the line of houses, following the white blazes back to the parking lot and arriving at 4.9 miles.

Hike 29 **Big Gunpowder Falls, Gunpowder Falls State Park, Harford County**

Type: walk	**Distance:** 4.1 miles
Rating: 4	**Time:** 2 hours
GPS: 39° 25.658'N, 76° 26.638'W	**Elevation change:** 375 feet
Best time: any time	**Best lenses:** 20mm to 100mm
Difficulty: moderate	

Directions: From the intersection of US-1 and MD-152, south of Bel Air, take US-1 south for 5.4 miles and turn left into a large parking area just before you cross the river. GPS coordinates: 39° 25.658'N, 76° 26.638'W.

On an initially heavily overcast day, I set out for some photographic fun at this section of Gunpowder Falls State Park, which is a thoroughly delightful urban oasis. Instead of rain, the clouds broke and the day dawned clear and bright, so I left my camera in my car and went for a wonderful sunrise trail run. Regardless of your goal, the vast trail network at Gunpowder Falls has something for everyone.

Begin by heading through the parking area, with the river on your right, to the overflow parking area. Go down some stairs, turning left onto the blue-blazed River Trail. In .4 miles, the yellow-blazed Sawmill Loop will join from the left; you'll hit it again at .7 miles. (We'll hit the side trails on the return.) After crossing Broad Run, just after the second Sawmill Loop junction, you can open up your stride and hoof it to 1.0 miles and Pot Rocks.

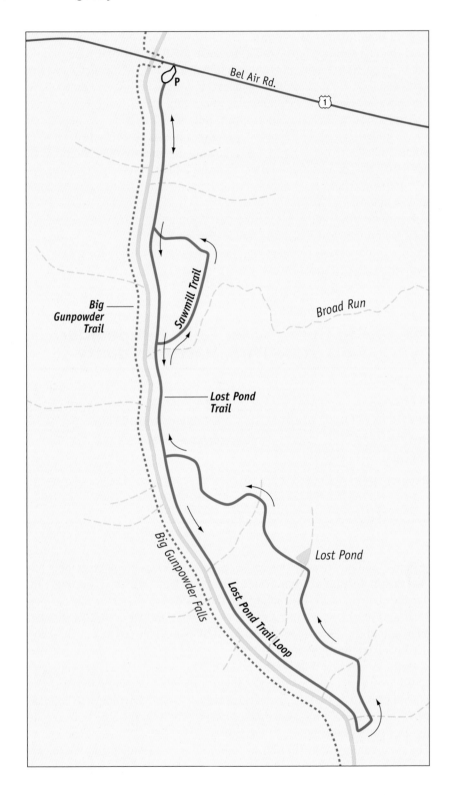

Bel Air Rd.

1

Broad Run

Big
Gunpowder
Trail

Sawmill Trail

Lost Pond
Trail

Big Gunpowder Falls

Lost Pond

Lost Pond Trail Loop

Here you can rock hop—very carefully—across the exposed Perry Hall Gneiss slabs well into the river. The potholes are formed by eddies that cause hammer stones to swirl around and drill down into the rock. The bigger the hole, the bigger the hammer stones. In autumn, views upstream and downstream are outstanding. Note that the Lost Pond Loop Trail joins here.

Stick to the riverside trail for another .9 miles (now at 1.6 miles) and swing uphill along No Name Stream to head away from the river. I-95 will be clearly audible.

Climbing easily before swinging left, the trail undulates up and down as it tries to maintain a level line. You'll hit Lost Pond, which is now just a muddy, successional meadow, at 2.2 miles. I looked around for wildflowers, but since I was here after the leaves came out, I was a couple weeks too late. If you're careful with your footing you can work around the meadow edge, shooting as you go.

Continue along the blue-blazed trail, making sometimes steep but generally casual descents toward the river. The unnamed run alongside has some nice little drops and burbles in it. It's particularly photogenic in the first 200 yards or so. If it hadn't been such a beautiful day, I probably would have filled my memory card just in this short section. Oh, how I wish it had been raining!

Rejoin the riverside trail at 2.8 miles and go right. When you hit Broad Run again at 3.3 miles, go right on the yellow Sawmill Trail, which quickly swings left to climb steeply. After a relatively mild section it goes left again to drop headlong over rocks and scree back to the Gunpowder River. Go right when you get back to the river at 3.7 miles, then start your cool-down phase, arriving back at your car at 4.1 miles. This is lovely running.

Hike 30 **Kilgore Falls, Rocks State Park, Harford County**

Kilgore Falls

Type: fall	**Difficulty:** easy
Rating: 5	**Distance:** .6 miles
GPS: 39° 41.467'N, 76° 25.633'W	**Time:** 30 minutes
Stream: Falling Branch of Deer Creek	**Elevation change:** 140 Feet
Height: 17 feet	**Best lenses:** 20mm to 70mm

Directions: From US-1 in Bel Air, take MD-24 north for 9.8 miles, passing through Rocks State Park, to the roundabout at MD-165 in the hamlet of Bushs Corner. Continue north on MD-24 for another 1.4 miles, then turn left onto St. Mary's Road. A partially collapsed white house marks the turn. Merge onto Clermont Mill Road in .5 miles. Pass a church on the right, then make an immediate right onto Falling Branch Road and enter the parking lot on the right in .2 miles. The lot is gated and doesn't open until 9:00 A.M. March to October; after that, it doesn't open until 10:00 A.M. It always closes at sunset and once your car is in, it's in. GPS coordinates: 39° 41.407'N, 76° 25.398'W.

Proceed down the gently sloping gravel path toward the creek. The trail rises and falls slightly until it settles in above the creek at .2 miles. Come to a Y at .25 miles and bear left, crossing the creek on concrete stepping

Kilgore Falls. I committed a pretty big photographic sin—I left my tripod in the car. This handheld, two-image panoramic was necessary to get the white fan of water to rest pleasingly in the large expanse of rock to the fall's right. *Canon EOS 5D Mkii, Canon 20-105L, polarizer, ISO100 setting, f4 @ 1/10s*

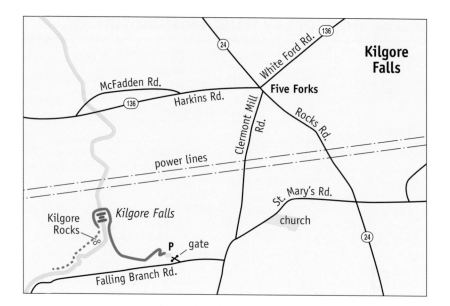

stones (some of which are partially submerged). Bear right to head to the falls, which you'll get to at .3 miles.

Kilgore is the most picturesque of Maryland's falls. The algae-covered rock face of the 17-foot cliff-edge drop is surrounded by large boulders and rock slabs that make a pleasing frame for the fall, and many of which provide nice shooting perches. The plunge pool near the fall is rather deep, but the broader tailwater is shallow enough for knee boots or hip waders. Shots from downstream are limited by an overhang on the right that covers a good portion of the fall's face. You'll need to be on the right-hand bank to get the best portrait-like shots.

If the downstream crossing isn't passable, continue upstream from the Y along the creek's left-hand side and cross using substantial stones about 20 yards above the drop. To get back below the fall, follow a fissure with a natural staircase to the small bench below.

Hike 31 **Rock Creek Park, Washington, DC**

Type: hike	**Distance:** 10.2 miles
Rating: 5	**Time:** 4 hours
GPS: 38° 56.368'N, 77° 3.14'W	**Elevation change:** 1,000 feet
Best time: any time	**Best lenses:** 17mm to 200mm
Difficulty: difficult	

Directions: From I-495 exit 30 on the north side of Washington, DC, exit onto US-29 south (Coleville Road). In 1.8 miles come to a traffic circle where 16th Street comes in from the left (an-odd looking green sculpture will be ahead). Carefully enter the circle and go left (south) on 16th Street. In 2.9 miles, bear right onto Blagden Avenue, which runs parallel to Colorado Avenue. In about .8 miles, Blagden swings right to enter the park. After 1.0 miles, turn left onto Beach Drive NW; Rock Creek will be on the right. In .3 miles, make a hard right onto Tilden Street NW, cross Rock Creek, and make a left onto Shoemaker Street NW as you come even with Pierce Mill on your right. Park in the lot on the left. If the lot is full, continue ahead and park on the left side of Shoemaker Street (facing downhill). GPS coordinates: 38° 56.368'N, 77° 3.14'W.

Rock Creek can be crowded on any weekend, especially during the first warm days of spring. That's fine—this 10.2-mile loop puts you on some lesser-used areas and has enough to keep the interest of any experienced hiker. On my first trip, I ran the loop and was pleasantly surprised by not only the beauty, but also by the "remoteness" of it. Here I was in the heart of the capital, with every parking lot filled, and yet I never saw more than a few people within my sightlines. What follows is not a shooting expedition, however, but rather a long outing with friends or family. To shoot the park, use Beach Drive NW heading north and park in one of the many pullouts, working the lovely creek in sections. The park is open dawn until dusk, with weekend closures of Beach Drive as well as Friday closures before a holiday. It's easiest to navigate on weekdays.

From Pierce Mill/Shelter #1, face the creek and turn right on a paved path running parallel and heading downstream. This is the Western Ridge Trail. Quickly come to a bridge on the left and make a right, walking away from the creek for a few yards (the pavilion will be off to the right). Make a hard left over a small footbridge that crosses a little run known as the Hazen Branch. After crossing, look for signage indicating a choice of trails—strenuous goes straight and moderate goes uphill to the right. Go straight and navigate the boot path that goes up and down the narrow ledges above Rock Creek. Descend around .25 miles, arriving at Bluff Bridge at .4 miles. Cross and go left, now on the blue-blazed Valley Trail.

Follow the paved trail for about .1 miles to near .5 miles and turn right at a small wooden sign in front of a few stairs. Climb the stairs, scamper across

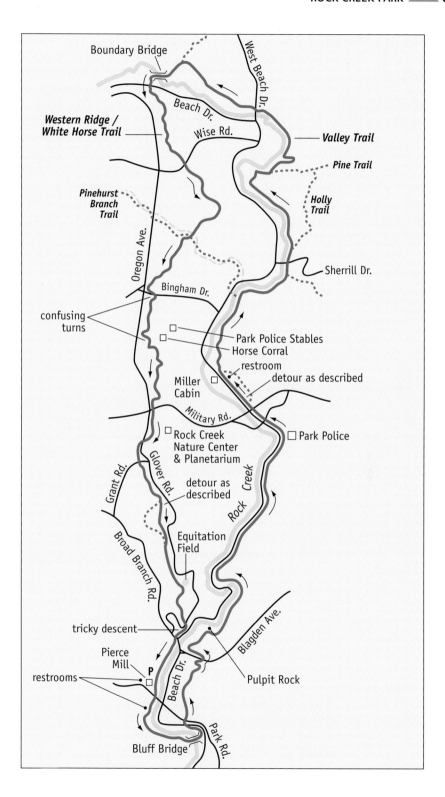

Boundary Bridge

West Beach Dr.

Beach Dr.

**Western Ridge /
White Horse Trail**

Wise Rd.

Valley Trail

Pine Trail

**Pinehurst
Branch
Trail**

**Holly
Trail**

Oregon Ave.

Sherrill Dr.

Bingham Dr.

confusing
turns

Park Police Stables
Horse Corral

restroom
detour as described

Miller
Cabin

Military Rd.

Rock Creek
Nature Center
& Planetarium

Park Police

Grant Rd.

Glover Rd.

detour as
described

Rock Creek

Broad Branch Rd.

Equitation
Field

tricky descent

Blagden Ave.

Pierce
Mill

P

restrooms

Beach Dr.

Pulpit Rock

Park Rd.

Bluff Bridge

Beach Drive, climb steeply up a gravel trail, and then cross Park Road. Continue to climb and arrive at a junction where the Meadow Trail goes left. Continue ahead, still climbing, and rejoin the meadow trail at .8 miles. Climb some more and pass a spur trail on the right that leads to Upshur Street. Continue on the blue-blazed trail, now with intermittent blazes, then descend rapidly. Shortly after, the trail makes a hard left and comes to a T at .9 miles. The trail ahead drops to Beach Drive; turn right to go to Blagden Avenue.

Cross Blagden Avenue at 1.28 miles, swing left to climb again, and then go right. Arrive at Pulpit Rock at 1.6 miles to find a leaves-off view looking upstream. Now drop to creek level where the pleasant trail descends as it swings left. Beach Drive is in view across the creek, as is a road bridge in the distance. Start another climb-and-drop sequence and pass a side trail on the left to Picnic Area #4 at 2.1 miles.

With Beach Drive on your side the trail is now more or less level all the way to Military Road. There is one minor climb as you approach the tennis center, and then a fence pushes the trail back to the left and downhill again. I had an encounter on this little downhill part with one of trail running's three worst critters: the dreaded root snake. I broke a toe on an exposed root but managed to finish the loop, although slowly. (In case you're wondering, the other two are the infamous rock squirrel and the vicious stump bunny. They are exceptionally nasty animals.)

Arrive at the Park Police Station at 3.0 miles; Picnic Area #5 is ahead near Joyce Road. You'll have to carefully—very carefully—cross Joyce Road, then head under the high bridge carrying Military Road over Rock Creek. After passing under Military Road at 3.14 miles, don't bother trying to find the blue blaze that heads right to the switchback uphill (as shown on the NPS map). Instead, go straight along Beach Drive to the bathrooms near Picnic Area #6 and the Miller Cabin. Here, you can fill water bottles. A few yards past the bathrooms, follow the little footpath that goes right, and hit the blue blaze a dozen yards later. Go left.

As you move along, the golf course will be out of view to the right and you'll see a "No Trespassing" sign behind the green for #14. Shortly after, the Black Horse Trail joins from the left at 3.5 miles. Arrive at Rolling Meadow Bridge at 3.8 miles. Pause here and walk to the bridge's middle for a nice view of Rock Creek. Return to the trail and continue north, passing the Whittier Trail at 4.1 miles, then pass under the Sherrill Drive Bridge at 4.2 miles.

The trail is flat from here to Boundary Bridge and parking area CT 1, running along a mud bank several feet above the creek. There are numerous little jogs, twist, side trails, and braids, so stick with the widest and most-used path. Whether running or walking, you can set a brisk pace, even if the surface is muddy. From Sherrill Drive you'll pass the Holly and Pine Trails at 4.3 and 4.9 miles, respectively. The blue-blazed trail makes an odd loop away from Rock Creek just north of the Pine Trail at 5.0 miles. The next landmark is West Beach Drive at 5.5 miles; pass under it and bear left just before CT 1 on a side trail. Arrive at Boundary Bridge and CT 1 at 6.1 miles.

The relatively flat half of the hike over, it's now time for some hills. As you exit CT 1, scamper across Beach Drive and head uphill on the green-blazed Western Ridge/White Horse Trail. The first pitch tops out at 6.5 miles to drop a few feet into a tiny creek, then climbs again, crossing Wise Drive at 6.7 miles and topping out at 6.77 miles. The trail surface is an old woods road that has had some gravel added over the years; however, there is some fist-sized scree in areas where the trail is incised, so if you're running, keep to the smoother edges.

Now descending, pass a Y on the left for Riley Spring Bridge at 6.9 miles, then begin a long, swinging right, passing an unmarked trail on the left at 7.0 miles. Continue to descend and drop into the Pinehurst Branch at 7.23 miles, cross the yellow-blazed Pinehurst Branch Trail, and climb again. The trail jogs right, then left through an intersection with trail CT 3 at 7.4 miles. Stick with the intermittent green blazes.

As you approach the large intersection of Oregon, Nebraska, and Bingham, a trail joins from the right at 7.55 miles. As you drop into the intersection, a paved path swings left and down, while a footpath goes straight, crossing Bingham at the light.

This next sequence can be confusing; I ended up doing it twice, and I had a map. Bear left, following the paved path downhill, and arrive at Bingham several dozen yards east of the traffic light. Do not take the footpath that stays on Bingham's north side. Look for a pullout/parking area across the road (this is Picnic Area 12), cross Bingham, bear slightly right around PIC 12, and find a paved path that heads steeply uphill through rhododendrons. Follow the paved path uphill and T into an access road for the Park Police Stables, now at 7.85 miles.

Ahead will be a large fenced garden, and near that will be a lone white bollard with a green blaze. Go left, then right onto a grassy area between the garden on your right and the horse corrals on your left. When you get to the woods, turn left, pass the corrals on your left, and then bear right to enter the woods, now at 7.9 miles. Drop a little and cross a seasonal run. Immediately after, the CT 5 connector joins from the left. Climb uphill, looping left as you go, and at 8.3 miles the White Horse Trail goes left at a T. You'll head right toward Oregon Avenue, then left, crossing Military Road at the traffic light at 8.35 miles. Climb to the Nature Center, where you can get water.

The trail passes through the Nature Center parking area. Follow signs for the Western Ridge Trail that takes you away from the building. Here, the trail drops quickly and crosses a road at PIC 14, then crosses Glover Road at PIC 13. With Glover above and to the left, descend and cross Grant Road at 8.71 miles. Join the White Horse Trail again at PIC 16 at 8.93 miles in an open field. As you exit the field, the green-blazed Western Ridge goes hard right;

instead, go straight on the White Horse Trail and rejoin the green-blazed trail at PIC 19 at 9.26 miles.

With Glover Road audible on the left, a large paddock (Equitation Field) appears on the left near 9.4 miles. As you approach, go right to follow the green blazes, then make a quick left to stay on the White Horse Trail. It's an odd turn that doesn't feel right if you're running. Now, begin a tricky descent and pop out onto Glover Road at PIC 27. Look across Glover Road for a stairwell partially hidden by a guardrail; it will be near where the guardrail begins. *Carefully* cross the blind curve and pitch off the road to drop like a rock. When you get to the next road, Broad Branch, stop to get your bearings. The Y-shaped intersection has a number of unmarked footpaths crossing it. Slightly to your right is an access road to a parking area. Quickly cross Broad Branch and follow this road, then ease left to get onto a paved path next to the creek. Follow this and pass under Park Road near the Pierce Mill at 10.1 miles, returning to your parking area at 10.2 miles.

I think you'll agree that this is a lovely walk or a challenging trail run, and that you'd never know you're only about 5 miles from Capitol Hill.

Hike 32 Great Falls, Chesapeake & Ohio Canal National Historic Park, Montgomery County

Type: chute	**Difficulty:** difficult
Rating: 5+	**Distance:** 4 miles
GPS: 38° 59.917'N, 77° 15.283'W	**Time:** 2 hours
Stream: Potomac River	**Elevation change:** 244 feet
Height: 76 feet	**Best lenses:** 50 mm to 400mm
Best time: any time	

Directions: From I-495 exit 41 on the west side of Washington, DC, exit onto the Clara Barton Parkway, heading west and following signs for Carderock and Great Falls. The parkway ends in 1.5 miles, just after passing the famed U.S. Navy research labs on the right (look for the Patriot missile battery). Turn left onto MacArthur Boulevard and follow it for 3.4 miles into the huge parking lot for Great Falls. GPS coordinates: 39° 0.086'N, 77° 14.844'W.

This 4-mile loop passes the famed falls and incorporates the northern section of the famous, popular, and often crowded Billy Goat Trail. The return portion of the loop uses the C&O canal towpath and is the same path that passes below you at Point Lookout (see Hike 52) in Garret County. The canal is hugely popular with local and long-distance bikers alike, plus runners of every type, and for good reason—it's well maintained and flat. The visitor center is open from 9:00 A.M. to 4:30 P.M., and the park grounds are open during daylight hours.

From the visitor center and historical tavern, cross the footbridge over Lock 20 and go left, putting the canal on your left. Walk .52 miles to a stop lock where the path is "closed." Turn right onto Billy Goat Trail A, which

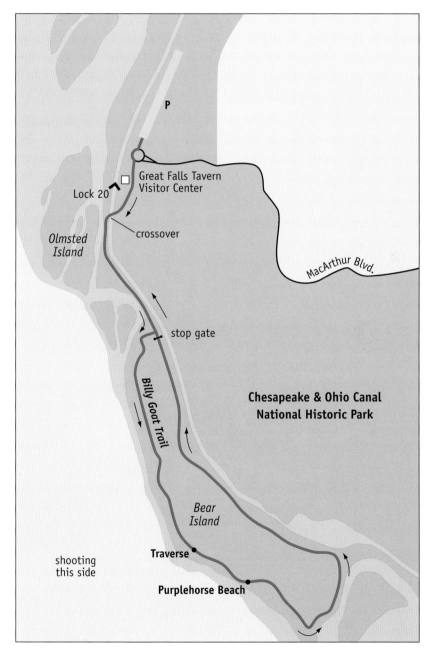

begins as a wide dirt path. You'll encounter the real Billy Goat Trail shortly at .55 miles where a series of pale blue blazes lead through very rocky terrain. Now it's time to have some fun! I should really get a t-shirt made that says: "I ♥ Boulders."

At .62 miles the trail swings a surprising left (a reroute), so keep an eye out for blazes. A little side trail blazed dark blue/white is found at .76 miles; this 20-yard diversion takes you to a nice exposure overlooking Mather Gorge below Great Falls. Look for rock climbers on the cliff face across the river in Virginia. Return to the main trail and continue downstream. The trail hangs close to the gorge edge, so it's a good idea to explore every little viewpoint to see what can be seen. Hopefully you'll see some of the osprey that ply the pools and eddies below the falls, looking for the easy meals that stunned fish provide.

Come to a warning sign at 1.05 miles, read it, and assess your fitness level. I think it's a little overzealous, but then again, there are people who simply aren't comfortable on the short pitch that's coming up at 1.3 miles.

As you move along the gnarly bit of fun that is the shattered rock surface, take a moment to observe the vegetation within the fissures and joints. Every crevice is a little ecosystem unto itself. If you have macro gear this will be heaven, even if there's not a single flat surface to set a tripod. The potholes—the round-bottomed things that look like they've been made by a

Great Falls. Great Falls is best shot from the Virginia side. This bight sunny day didn't detract from the scene, I think, although I would have preferred something by full moon light. Post–Superstorm Sandy video from this location showed no discernible fall; rather, it looked like a large rapid that dropped 40 feet at most. *Canon EOS 5D Mkii, Canon 20-105L, polarizer, ISO100 setting, f16 @ 1/8s*

giant drill—were formed by moving water. Take a moment to consider that. You're standing on what was the river bed during the last ice age, and you're how high above the gorge now?

After a short sequence of interesting rock traverses, make a woodsy descent, arriving at the grandiosely named "50 Foot Traverse" at 1.3 miles. This side-wise climb follows a steep crack back to the cliff top. It's best to lean into the wall on the left and to always keep three points of contact with the rock face at all times. Also, this is not a fun place to be in rain, and it's downright dangerous in icing conditions. You'll hit "Midway Exit" at 1.5 miles; avail yourself if need be. Next, you'll drop again and come to a wide beach, called Purplehorse Beach, at 1.55 miles. Cross, and as you do, bear slightly left to follow a blaze near the trees. Swing left at 1.66 miles, heading down a rock fall, and at last put your feet back on dirt. To your right is a large pool where you'll see some faded gray blazes (which are painted over blue)—don't follow them, as these will lead you astray. Look around for brighter blue blazes and follow those.

At 1.76 miles come to a lovely lily pad–filled slack water section of a stream on the left, then turn left and cross a footbridge. Go left at a side trail to an overlook, found at 1.95 miles. Drop into a seasonal drainage that may be impassable during a spring flood or after heavy weather. Climb out on the muddy trail at 2.0 miles and swing left above a large slack-water slough that separates Bear Island from Sherwin Island. Carefully follow the blue-blazed trail as it climbs, then drops three times. Exit Billy Goat A onto the canal towpath at 2.28 miles. It's hiker's choice as to whether you want to head back to your car on the towpath or cross the canal and follow the Overlook Trail. On a brutally hot August day, I took the easy way out and followed the tow path. Head left (the canal will be on your right) and make your way back to your car, arriving at 4.0 miles.

Don't forget the fall overlooks and the loop around Olmstead Island. You can't shoot the falls from this side, at least not well—for that you'll need to be on the Virginia side. To get there, head back down the Clara Barton Parkway, get on I-495, cross the Potomac, and take exit 44 to follow VA-193 (Georgetown Pike) toward Langley. In 4.2 miles, bear right onto Old Dominion Drive, following signs for Great Falls Park, and park in the large lot past the visitor center. GPS coordinates: 38° 59.997′N, 77° 15.412′W. The bookstore/visitor center is open from 10:00 A.M. to 5:00 P.M., and the park is open from 7:00 A.M. to 5:00 P.M.

Follow a graded trail, passing the visitor center, then follow signs to Overlooks 1, 2, and 3. It's about a 1.4-mile round trip. All the overlooks are nice and provide views facing the falls. You can shoot all manner of images, from wide angle to long as well as panoramic. Look for kayakers in brightly colored boats plying the tailwater. The falls are obviously best in the high water of spring, say mid-April; flow can be hit or miss, depending on mountain snowpack. For fall color, you'll need a wet summer or a tropical storm

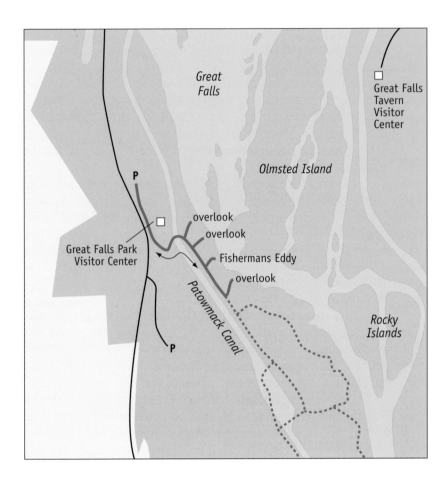

to put enough water in the fall to get that awesome raging flow. Winter snow would be nice as well. A shot of the falls by the full moon would be spectacular. I never got the chance to try this, and since the gate closes at 5:00 P.M., you'll have to park along VA-193 at one of the Old Carriage Trails, aka the second Difficult Run trailhead, and walk in; as it's a nearly 3-mile round trip by headlamp, this is not for the novice hiker.

Hike 33 **Patuxent Research Refuge North Tract, Anne Arundel County**

Type: hike	**Distance:** 10.6 miles
Rating: 5	**Time:** 4 hours
GPS: 39° 4.677'N, 76° 46.324'W	**Elevation change:** 494 feet
Best time: morning	**Best lenses:** 17mm to 200mm
Difficulty: moderate	

Directions: From I-95 exit 34 south of Baltimore, take MD-32 east toward US-1. In 5.8 miles take exit 8 for MD-198 toward Laurel Fort Meade Road. Keep right as you get to the top of the ramp and take the first exit right as you enter a round-about. In .9 miles turn left onto Bald Eagle Drive as you pass some ball fields (there'll be a large brown sign). The gate ahead opens at 8:00 A.M. Drive .9 miles to the refuge headquarters on the left and park here. You MUST register at the office. GPS coordinates: 39° 4.677'N, 76° 46.324'W.

This road hike is popular with runners of all types. In fact, that's all I saw during my hot August loop. You know elite runners when you see them—they're the ones putting down a blistering pace without any effort—and I saw a bunch.

The Patuxent North Tract used to be a part of Fort Meade and was an active army training unit during the Vietnam War. You must register and fill out a "hold harmless waiver" because there's still unexploded ordnance around. Clean-up and restoration activities are ongoing, so it's a good idea to call ahead to check for any area closures: (301) 776-3090 or www.fws .gov/northeast/patuxent/ntintro.html. The refuge is open from 8:00 A.M. to 4:00 P.M., with the last pass issued at 3:30 P.M. You must be off the property at 4:00 P.M.; if you're not, FWS will come looking for you. Weekend hours

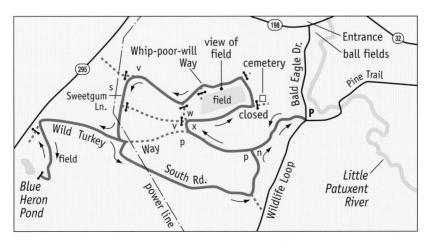

Reeves Pond. It's maybe an acre, but Reeves Pond is a lovely little lily-filled pond. Walk the entire perimeter, shooting verticals and horizontals as you go. *Canon EOS 5D Mkii, Canon 20-105L, polarizer, ISO100 setting, f16 @ 1/10s*

are 8:00 A.M. to 7:00 P.M. from mid-June to August. Typically the Lake Allen Road is closed during the week, and the Wildlife Loop is closed to public access between Cattail Pond and Bailey Marsh. When you leave the office, don't forget to put the yellow permit copy on your dash and keep the pink copy with you at all times.

From the office, head out on the Forest Trail, which begins as the board-walk across the road from the office. Turn left at .12 miles when you get to a sign for Wild Turkey Way and come to a gravel road at .18 miles. Go right on the road. Arrive at a signed intersection at .52 miles; to the left is King Fisher Road to Reeves Pond, your return route. Continue ahead on Wild Turkey Way and come to a Y at 1.13 miles. Bear right onto Sweet Gum Lane, then come to another Y at 1.29 miles where you'll go right onto Whip-poor-will Way. You're now heading back toward the office.

After a boring series of short climbs the road swings left (to head north) at 1.98 miles, and you'll pass an old cemetery on the right. This is Cemetery #10, the Biggs (Anderson)-Waters Cemetery. The oldest grave is that of John

Waters, who died in 1771, followed by his wife Mary Ijams Waters in 1773. Another cemetery is west of the drop zone (at 2.3 miles), but I couldn't find it. There are several others scattered throughout the North Tract. When you get back to office, ask to see the desk copy of *Rediscovering the North Tract: An Anne Arundel County Time Capsule.* It's some interesting reading.

In a little while, come to a vast, open field on the left. The road will then swing left to head west, now at 2.29 miles, along the field's north side. This is the Dean K. Phillips parachute drop zone. Look for a small monument on the curve's inside edge. When you get to around 2.57 miles, look for a little lane that heads left, go left, and in a few yards find a concrete pad on the right. This is the high ground overlooking the drop zone; if you have a big lens with you, this is the place to use it. GPS coordinates: 39° 4.925'N, 76° 47.329'W.

Return to the road, go left, and shortly after reenter the woods. At 3.1 miles, come to another Y where left makes a quick return to Wild Turkey Way and right continues along Sweet Gum Lane toward Blue Heron Pond. Go right. After a long straight section interspersed with fields on the right, hang a hard left at 3.67 miles to run parallel with power lines. MD-295 will be audible but out of view to the right. Pass under the power lines at 4.21 miles. Wild Turkey Way will be visible to the left as you descend slightly to arrive at it at 4.35 miles. Examine the intersection—you're at a T with a brown bench, and to the left is a Y. Now walk along Wild Turkey Way past a bench to head for Blue Heron Pond.

Wild Turkey Way swings left (to head south) at 5.2 miles, within sight of MD-295. Pass through a gate into Area T at 5.6 miles. Ahead are more large open fields. Swing right to reenter woods at 5.84 miles and arrive at Blue Heron Pond at 6.0 miles. A poorly placed photo blind is to the right of the gate ahead of you; however, there is a nice bench just beyond. On the stifling August morning I got here, access to the pond was closed, which was rather upsetting. It's a good-sized detention basin with a healthy forest, and beyond that would be the perfect fall color shot.

Reverse your route and head back to the dark brown bench you passed at 4.35 miles. Now, at 7.53 miles, bear right onto South Road and head for Reeves Pond. Pass under the power lines again at 8.02 miles, and at 8.32 miles pass a road to the right for areas M, Q, and LZ-2. At 9.02 miles, arrive at a T with King Fisher Road, go left, and in a few yards arrive at the lovely lily pad–filled Reeves Pond. Find the bench, have a seat, and watch the dragonflies cast about for a meal or a mate. Also look for turtles sunning themselves on one of several logs. This little pond was the highlight for me. You can work around the pond in both directions, trying compositions as you go.

When you've had your fill, continue north along King Fisher Road and T into Wild Turkey Way at 9.3 miles. Go right, then left on the Forest Trail at 10.48 miles. Arrive back at your car at 10.6 miles and check out at the office by returning both the yellow and pink copies of your permit.

Hike 34 Merkle Wildlife Sanctuary, Prince George's County

Type: hike	**Distance:** 5.7 miles
Rating: 4+	**Time:** 2 hours
GPS: 38° 43.650'N, 76° 42.519'W	**Elevation change:** 244 feet
Best time: morning	**Best lenses:** 17mm to 400mm
Difficulty: moderate	

Directions: From I-495 exit 11 on the southeast side of Washington, DC, near Andrews AFB, take MD-4 south (Pennsylvania Avenue) for about 2.8 miles and exit onto MD-223 (Woodyard Road) for Clinton and Melwood. At the bottom of the ramp, bear right onto MD-223, and in .2 miles turn left at the light onto Marlboro Pike. Marlboro will make a long right, and when you get to South Osborne in .5 miles go straight to keep with it. Osborne is a curvy country road. After 2.3 miles, T into US-301. Go left here and make an immediate right onto MD-382. There are traffic lights, so don't worry. Follow MD-382 south for 4.0 miles, then bear left off of it onto St. Thomas Church Road. In 2.2 miles St. Thomas Church Road swings hard right to become Fenno Road, which you'll follow for another .7 miles before turning left at a small sign onto the sanctuary property. Follow the one-way loop to the visitor center and park in the large lot. GPS coordinates: 38° 43.650'N, 76° 42.519'W.

Merkle Wildlife Sanctuary has several limitations, imposed when the property was deeded to the state. The hike as described is closed between October 1 and December 31 to allow geese to roost. Also, the visitor center hours vary from season to season based on area closures and school group usage. Generally speaking, the property is open from 7:00 A.M. until sunset. For current hours and closures, visit http://www.dnr.state.md .us/publiclands/southern/merkle.asp.

Begin your hike by walking along the road, passing the visitor center on the right and heading for the barns and silo. As I passed by the silo, a pair of osprey bolted from the nest on top. They circled a couple times, screaming all the while, but after several orbits they calmed down and landed again. That's when I spied two chicks in the nest.

At .3 miles go right on a gravel road toward the red barn. When you get to "traffic circle" or Y at .71 miles, go left and begin the loop that uses a good portion of the Critical Area Driving Tour (CADT). Swing right at 1.2 miles toward the woods, then arrive at a red gate at 1.3 miles. Bear right around the gate and walk along an older, grassy woods road. A small wooden sign on the right announces a CADT parking area. Next, arrive at an observation tower at 1.5 miles. This substantial tower overlooks a swamp feeding the Patuxent River. Linger a while and then return to the main road, arriving around 1.6 miles, and go right again to continue your loop.

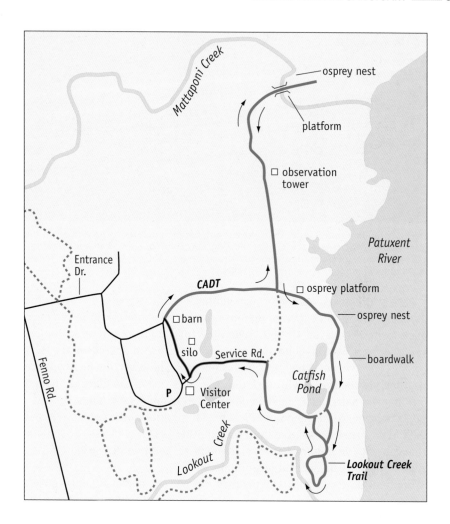

Exit the sanctuary property for Patuxent River State Park when you get to the huge boardwalk bridge at 2.1 miles. To your left is an osprey nest, which had a lone female and chick when I was here. Not knowing what wildlife shooting opportunities there were here, I left my big lens in the car—what a mistake! This is the only nest around where you're slightly above it so the shooting position is perfect, plus the birds are habituated due to all the canoe/kayak traffic, so they'll remain in place the whole time. You'll need some big glass, like a 400mm or longer.

Continue on the boardwalk to the large tower, now at 2.92 miles. Finish this out-and-back portion by crossing the boardwalk bridge to the pavement, then turn around. On my return to finish the loop, I moved several small turtles from the road. They weren't in any real danger, although I was concerned about inattentive bike riders.

From Mattaponi Creek Bridge. There were a number of people going up and down the glassy waters of Mattaponi Creek. After shooting a dozen or so, I settled on this pair of yellow kayaks. Note the osprey nest in the background to the right. *Canon EOS 5D Mkii, Canon 20-105L, polarizer, ISO100 setting, f8 @ 1/40s*

Pass both towers, and when you get back to the exposed field with the traffic circle you can either go right to head back to your car, or left to head back toward the river. Go left. When the road swings right at 3.9 miles, you'll see an old photo blind and an osprey nest close to this side of the river bank in open water. The photo blind is unusable; however, the nearby fence with the plywood on it will work fine. Stay this side of the fence. Although they may be habituated, one should never press raptors too hard. They can easily be spooked to the point of leaving the nest for hours, which will put the chick at risk from predators or hypothermia. If a raptor's behavior changes, you've gotten too close. Remember: good wildlife photography takes immense patience and lots of time.

Continue down the trail with the river on your left, and at 4.0 miles go left onto a boardwalk trail marked by a large sign kiosk. Come to a view platform that puts you between two osprey nests. Return to the gravel road and go left, then right for Catfish Pond. Catfish Pond is actually a slough, and its inky black waters are prime duck habitat, but, nobody was home during my noon-time sojourn. Return to the road again and go right. At 4.5 miles arrive at the Lookout Creek Trail on the left and go left. This is a .75-mile figure 8 loop through the woods.

To complete the figure 8 go left at the first Y at 4.56 miles, then shortly after go left again at the next Y. When you arrive at the creek at 4.75 miles, the trail swings right to run parallel to it. When you get to a T at 4.9 miles go left again, then at the next junction (you guessed it), go left. Pop out of the trees and hit a hard right, then go left to rejoin the gravel road at 5.02 miles.

The road makes a series of left-right chicanes, and at 5.35 miles arrives at a huge tree. To the left is an old "Road Closed" sign referring to CADT traffic. Go left, and at 5.53 miles come to a farm pond on the right. I spied several large snapping turtles moving through the grass. Return to your car at 5.7 miles.

Hike 35 Calvert Cliffs State Park, Calvert County

Type: hike	**Distance:** 4 miles
Rating: 4+	**Time:** 1 hour, 30 minutes
GPS: 38° 23.790'N, 76° 26.125'W	**Elevation change:** 500 feet
Best time: any time	**Best lenses:** 17mm to 200mm
Difficulty: moderate	

Directions: From I-495 exit 11 on the southeast side of Washington, DC, take MD-4 south (Pennsylvania Avenue) for 44.8 miles and turn left onto a short cutoff road, Hg Trueman Road, following signs for MD-765 and Calvert Cliffs State Park. In 300 feet cross MD-765 and pull into the large parking loop for the park. The lot will be crowded on any nice weekend, and you may have to cruise around for a spot. GPS coordinates: 38° 23.790'N, 76° 26.125'W.

This park is open from sunrise to sunset year round. There is a parking fee of $5 per car.

The trailhead is near the small detention basin or pond at the parking loop's south end. Head out along the red-blazed Beach of Cliff Trail, which joins a woods road only to turn off it at .31 miles. Quickly cross the yellow-blazed trail. The path becomes wide and sandy, so you can set a brisk pace. Next, pass the white-blazed trail at .7 miles.

Come to a slack-water pond or large meander in Grays Creek at 1.1 miles. This marshland is filled with lily pads and yellow iris, numerous standing snags, and more than a few curious turtles. From here to the beach you'll be along Gray's Creek, sometimes at water level and sometimes above. The marsh frogs (I don't know what species), were very active and noisy during

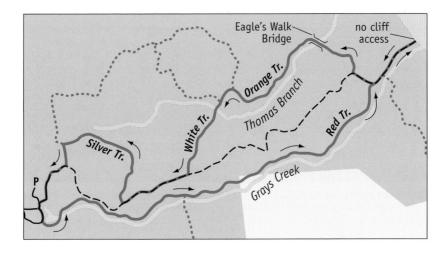

my visit. The marsh would be quiet, then slowly the calls of the frogs would crescendo to a loud cacophony, then more quickly decrescendo to silence. It was as if, by some sort of amphibian agreement, they all decided it had gotten loud enough and quieted down in unison. The calls were not the croaks or trills of most frogs; these were more like the distinct clicks of a Geiger counter delivering bad news to someone at the nearby nuclear plant.

The best overall view is when you finally turn right off the trail onto a gravel road at 1.45 miles. It's a tough shoot in full sun unless you're here very early or very late. The contrast between the north and south banks is too much. This place would be awesome in morning fog or mist.

When you finally begin to see lots of sky, you'll pass a small impoundment. This earthen dam separates the freshwater Grays Creek from the saltwater Chesapeake Bay. Shortly after, you'll arrive at the tiny beach and namesake cliffs at 1.71 miles. Access to the cliff base is closed due to landslides and slumps. Two things happen to the loose sand and clay. First, in rain events, the soil above the cliff face becomes saturated and large amounts of material slide off like a ribbon, creating a landslide. Second, wave action undercuts several feet of the cliff face and a large block of clay can just drop down—that's a slump. A number of people have been hurt

Grays Creek Marsh. This is one noisy place to take a photograph. Several places afford a nice shooting position; this one is close to a little check dam that keeps the freshwater marsh filled. *Canon EOS 5D Mkii, Canon 20-105L, polarizer, ISO100 setting, f8 @ 1/80s*

over the years by these events so, unfortunate as it is, access is forbidden. You also can't get to the cliff tops—don't try.

Reverse your route, and when you're back to where the red-blazed trail joined the road at 1.9 miles, go right up the service road instead of left. This will take you away from the herd path into quiet woods. At the hill crest, swing right onto the orange-blazed trail where the service road goes left, now at 2.0 miles. Descend the little ridge and cross over Eagle Walk Bridge at 2.1 miles. You're now at the head of Thomas Creek Bog. Notice all the downed trees with root balls still attached. This is what Hurricane Irene did in 2011, and man did she do a number on the place. Although the bog is sheltered and the winds here weren't too bad, the massive rainfall provided a one-two punch. Thomas Bog is impossible to shoot in full sun, even with High Dynamic Range (HDR) technology. For scenes like these, I find that HDR creates an unrealistic image that just wouldn't sell. Damp, misty conditions are best here.

Come to a Y at 2.6 miles where the orange-blazed trailheads right and an unsigned connector trail goes down and left. Go left to connect with the white-blazed trail. In 60 yards, come to a T where the white-blazed trail goes both up and right, and ahead and down. Go straight ahead on the white-blazed trail, descending slightly, then shortly after cross a small foot bridge over Thomas Creek at 2.7 miles. When you T into the access road at 2.92 miles, go right and pass the red-blazed connector trail on the left.

At 3.2 miles the silver trail T's in from the right. Go right, away from the road. The silver-blazed trail makes a very long, looping left through the woods. You'll T into a multicolored junction of red, silver, orange, and white blazes at 3.6 miles at the emergency siren indicated on the park map (the little black triangle). Road noise will be audible ahead of you. Go left on the now-sandy lane, and in 50 yards go right to join the gravel access road at an orange gate. This will dump you out at the north parking lot at 3.5 miles, which is about .2 miles from the south lot.

In this delightful woods environment, you just don't get a sense of the magnitude of development on the peninsula. Just 2.5 miles north is the Calvert Cliffs nuclear plant, which has two reactors generating about 1,600Mw of power. One mile south is the massive Dominion Cove LNG facility with a storage capacity of 7.8 billion cubic feet, and 7.5 miles south is the Patuxent River NAS. All this industry, and you would never know any of it was here. What a wonderful little park this is.

Hike 36 Chapman State Park, Charles County

Type: walk	**Distance:** 3.6 miles
Rating: 4	**Time:** 1 hour, 30 minutes
GPS: 38° 36.734'N, 77° 7.078'W	**Elevation change:** 294 feet
Best time: any time	**Best lenses:** 17mm to 200mm
Difficulty: easy	

Directions: From I-495 exit 3 on the south side of Washington, DC, take MD-210 south toward Indian Head. In 17.2 miles turn right onto the small side street of Mt. Aventine Road. When you T into Chapman Landing Road in .2 miles, turn left then make the first right onto a gravel lane/parking area. Don't block the gate. GPS coordinates: 38° 36.734'N, 77° 7.078'W.

This small gem of a park sits just 18 miles south of our nation's capitol and you'd never know—it feels that isolated by space and time. The Mount Aventine Tract contains an old estate house, now used as a lovely rental venue, and the remains of a small village. You can learn about the estate history on the DNR website or from http://chapmanforest.org/history_mtaventine.shtml.

Begin by heading up the wide gravel lane, and as buildings come into view pass the Coastal Woodlands Trail on the right at .27 miles. When you get to the start of the cedar-lined lane fronting the mansion, bear left onto

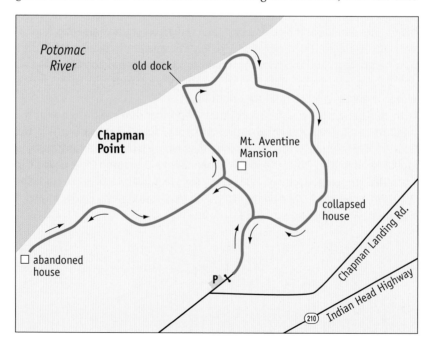

the Potomac River Trail at .33 miles. Pass the tobacco barn at .5 miles and shortly after, at .56 miles, come to a T with the Marsh Trail. Head left, following a mowed grass lane skirting a field, which you'll leave to enter the woods at .75 miles by going right, then left again. Here, the trail becomes a wide, grassy woods road that makes a series of casual meanders as the Potomac comes into view on the right near 1.1 miles. There are about 200 yards of marsh between you and the river, and it was here that I spotted a female wood duck and her chicks paddling around calmly—that is, until I scared them to death.

As you move along, the marsh slowly gives way to open water near 1.2 miles, finally meeting it at 1.25 miles. The trail kind of ends here, but feel free to pick your way along the bank to an old green house at 1.35 miles. There's a prominent "No Trespassing" sign and plenty of evidence that this is a bit of a party spot for boaters.

Reverse your route back to the T with the Marsh Trail, arriving at 2.1 miles. Right will now take you back to your car; instead, go straight toward the river. When the road swings right near 2.25 miles, a footpath appears and branches left. Go left and in a few yards pass a ruined cabin, then arrive again at the Potomac. Across from you is Virginia and Mason Neck NWR, and if you look to the right you can see tall buildings on the horizon in Alexandria. While jotting notes in my field journal, an eagle flew low and slow, its wings really clawing for lift as it trailed a chunk of rope or fishing equipment behind it. I couldn't tell if it was carrying this flotsam or had it tangled around a foot. I certainly hope it was the former. As you travel Maryland's tidewater country, you'll see fishing line recycling canisters (typically a long section of six-inch PVC pipe). These are very important to the survival of eagles, osprey, harriers, and kestrels as they remove monofilament line from the habitat. Sit for a while and enjoy the view.

Return to the main trail and go left to keep the river on your left. Arrive at a signed junction at 2.53 miles. Go left and join the Coastal Woodland Trail. At 3.05 miles, come to another T at an old homesite; the trail to the left is signed, whereas the trail ahead leads you out of the property. Go ahead and explore inside the old home. You'll find an upright clothes dryer, a couple stoves, and an old GE refrigerator . . . it's like an episode of *American Pickers*. The obvious question, however, is, why the low ceiling? As the foundation subsides into the soft ground the floor has remained stationary, so the ceiling has moved down. In a few decades, you won't even notice that there was a first floor.

Continue along the signed trail and pass another, even bigger building at 3.17 miles. The trail narrows a bit, then opens up again as you arrive at the main drive at 3.32 miles. Now go left and return to your car at 3.6 miles. All in all, it's a lovely way to spend a summer's day.

Hike 37 **Nelson Point, Charles County**

Type: walk	**Distance:** .6 miles
Rating: 3	**Time:** 30 minutes
GPS: 38° 34.761'N, 77° 8.247'W	**Elevation change:** 50 feet
Best time: morning	**Best lenses:** 17mm to 200mm
Difficulty: easy	

Directions: From I-495 exit 3 on the south side of Washington, DC, take MD-210 south toward Indian Head. In 17.9 miles turn left onto MD-225 east and in 1.6 miles bear right onto MD-224 (Chicamauxen Road). As you come to the double entrances to Henry Lackey Middle School, slow down as you move down a shallow grade and ease onto the shoulder after you pass the second entrance. At 1.1 miles from the turn onto MD-224 park on the right. GPS coordinates: 38° 34.761'N, 77° 8.274'W.

Before beginning, it's best to spray your boots with DEET, as ticks can be an issue here. Parking at the GPS coordinates will put you within 100 feet or less of the trailhead. The challenge is finding the actual trail through the dense grass along the road's shoulder. The shoulder will be above the forest floor, so look down and into the woods for two signs set about 80 feet into the forest. There'll be a brown "Adopt a Park" and "Audubon" sign on the left, and a silver/green sign on the right sitting just behind some dirt and gravel piles. You can walk on the shoulder if necessary. Once you find the signs, enter the woods and stand between the signs, carefully looking between them for an old white blaze on a tree. To the left of the blaze will be a wide grassy swath (most likely behind a blowdown). If you have a topo map or are using TOPO! Software, you are looking at the woods road that sits just west of the school. So far so good—you found the road.

Walk toward the grassy path behind the blowdown and after several paces the woods road reveals itself as a wide, grass-covered lane heading

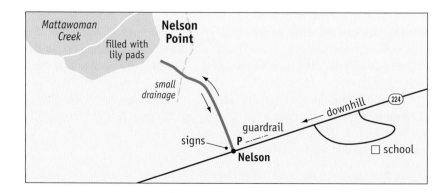

Nelson Point. Facing north, Nelson Point would be best during twilight, but unfortunately that simply wasn't workable for me. Although it would be nice in fall color, you'll have to be careful. The water plants don't display fall color—they go from green to dead brown—so getting a nice fall shot will require several trips. *Canon EOS 5D Mkii, Canon 20-105L, polarizer, ISO100 setting, f8 @ 1/80s*

through the trees. After a few dozen yards you'll spot an unused sign kiosk. The signage and kiosk were efforts to reopen the trail many years ago. Budget cuts of various amounts have slowed restoration to a glacial crawl. In fact, Audubon and the Sierra Club do a tremendous amount of work for DNR in this region. It would be hard to imagine how some of the parks along the Patuxent would function without the small army of committed volunteers. Move slowly along the old lane and within 100 yards the obvious path fades to nothing.

Be careful to follow the intermittent, faded white blazes. This is a seldom-used trail, so stick with basic trail craft by not walking too fast and always keeping one blaze in sight, whether ahead or behind. It's not easy, but it's certainly fun!

The trail encounters dense understory at .16 miles and begins to curve slowly left, where it starts to resemble a shallow depression or ditch. No blazes are found here, so follow the one and only path through the dense cover. Next, cross a muddy little run at .17 miles, and now look up to find a lone faded blaze ahead and slightly left. You'll climb a couple feet, daylight will peek through the forest ahead, and farther on you'll see water. Don't rush, take your time, and keep looking for blazes ahead and behind so you can spy your return path.

Arrive at the water's edge at .25 miles, GPS coordinates: 38° 34.761′N, 77° 8.274′W. Turn right and work your way around a series of blowdowns, keeping the river on the left. Just beyond these are three parallel depressions, like tire tracks. You should be able to see a white blaze on a massive hickory nearby. Follow the blaze. As the river curves away from the path, the path moves right and almost disappears into a tree tunnel. No blazes indicate this, but you'll be about 40 yards from the river, and once through the path just vaporizes. I spent a good twenty minutes trying to pick up an additional trail sign but couldn't. This is the end.

I found a comfortable log and quietly sat for several minutes atop the river bank. A refreshing breeze stirred the acres of water hyacinths filling the shallow river bend. A pileated woodpecker moved slowly closer until it noticed me, its alarm call shattering the silence. A pair of red-bellied woodpeckers began to call to each other and several mallards plied the hyacinths and swam ever closer while the calls of several geese came and went on the breeze. Movement to my left caught my attention, and as I turned, a large hawk swooped low over the river and disappeared into the trees, its flat-pitched scream slicing through the woods. A great blue heron settled onto its stilt-like legs for an afternoon snack. The best part of creating these guides for you is this simple act of being still. I don't mean sitting still, I mean *being* still. When you do that, the woods will come alive and the magic will come to you.

As you carefully reverse your route, look at the terrain around you and you'll notice some shallow ruts or several depressions that almost look like short lanes or roads, several dozen yards long. Now that you've experienced this place, it's time to understand what came before. About fifteen years ago, this was a junk car lot and the swampland of the river bend was filled with old wrecks. With an army of volunteer labor, the DNR pulled hundreds of cars out of the woods, and all the cars near the river bank they could get to. Who knows what's under the vast hyacinth blanket, but it can't be good.

Take your time heading back and keep a sharp eye for those blazes.

Hike 38 Sugarloaf Mountain Natural Area, Frederick County

White Rocks 1

Type: ledge	**Field of view:** 254° to 308°
Rating: 5+	**Relief:** 20 feet
GPS, parking: 39° 16.542′N, 77° 23.925′W	**Elevation difference:** 427 feet
GPS, vista: 39° 16.972′N, 77° 23.951′W	**Height:** 884 feet
Faces: 281°	

White Rocks 2

Type: ledge	**Field of view:** 274° to 312°
Rating: 5+	**Relief:** 35 feet
GPS, parking: 39° 16.542'N, 77° 23.925'W	**Elevation difference:** 562 feet
GPS, vista: 39° 17.021'N, 77° 23.982'W	**Height:** 884 feet
Faces: 294°	

East View

Type: ridge	**Field of view:** 100° to 160°
Rating: 4	**Relief:** 20 feet
GPS, parking: 39° 15.621'N, 77° 23.393'W	**Elevation difference:** 527 feet
GPS, vista: 39° 15.621'N, 77° 23.393'W	**Height:** 932 feet
Faces: 130°	

West View

Type: ridge	**Field of view:** 280° to 340°
Rating: 4	**Relief:** 30 feet
GPS, parking: 39° 15.611'N, 77° 23.881'W	**Elevation difference:** 538 feet
GPS, vista: 39° 15.611'N, 77° 23.881'W	**Height:** 947 feet
Faces: 310°	
Best time: sunrise through sunset	**Time:** 1 hour
Difficulty: moderate	**Elevation change:** 313 feet
Distance: 2.2 miles	**Best lenses:** 17mm to 200mm

Directions: From I-270 exit 22 southeast of Frederick, take MD-109 south/Old Hundred Road for 2.8 miles and turn right onto MD-95/Comus Road. In 2.9 miles, turn right again onto Mt. Ephraim Road. You'll pass through a small village, Sugarloaf Mountain Park, then head down a tree-lined drive and transition from pavement to gravel. After turning right onto Mt. Ephraim Road, go for 1.9 miles and park on the left where Mt. Ephraim Road makes a hard left over a small creek as a blue-blazed trail crosses. The sunken road is narrow with a couple of blind turns and dips, so go slowly. GPS coordinates: 39° 16.542'N, 77° 23.925'W.

This short in-and-out hike takes you to an amazing view in Frederick County. From the smallish parking area head several yards north up Mt. Ephraim Road to dark blue blazes on the right, and turn right into the woods. Now on a wide path, come to a signpost noting the North Peaks Trail. After .37 miles of steady but not difficult uphill, you enter a saddle-like area. To the right is the main 1,287-foot peak of Sugarloaf Mountain, ahead is another large hill, and to the left is a large knob.

Continue ahead, descend slightly, and then begin another steady climb. You'll reach the top at .65 miles in a rock garden. Pass through the boulders and ledges and make a hard left to pitch off the ridge for a few dozen yards and cross another saddle. Climb some more to find a signpost for White Rocks at .85 miles. Go left and arrive at the first outcrop at .9 miles.

There are two exposures, the one in front of you and the one to the left up the trail. This second exposure will be visible from the first. The view from this ledge looks upon rolling fields and is a lovely view of verdant farmland. There are a couple small houses that sit among the trees and thus won't be much of an issue. A small pine fronting the view to your right will be an issue, however, and you'll need to carefully check the edges of your frame.

The second view is a short distance from the first. Head north up the trail about 40 yards and turn left to the view. This ledge is better, photographically

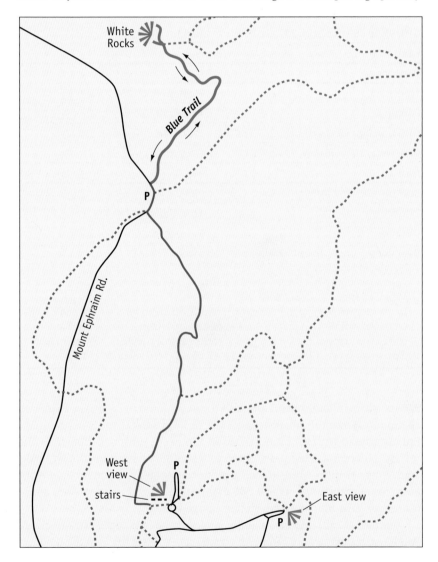

Sugar Loaf Mountain. The day after Thanksgiving blew bone-numbingly cold and the chill north wind came up the flank of Sugar Loaf Mountain like an icy bulldozer. Shot handheld, this monochrome image is what I call a record shot of someplace to return to. Fall color was thwarted by both Hurricane Irene and Superstorm Sandy, which was quite frustrating. *Canon EOS 5D Mkii, Canon 20-105L, polarizer, ISO100 setting, f8 @ 1/50s*

speaking, as it has more relief with no offending foreground trees. Some minor bouldering is needed to get to the best perch, which has a white patina of vulture poop—don't worry, it sounds nasty, but it's just like dried paint. This view also faces northwest and looks off toward Piner Rock and Mountville. The foreground is tree covered and begs to be shot in fall color. The valley to the north surrounding Urbana is completely open to the east; thus, this location will make for spectacular morning shots as dramatic sidelight fills the farmland ahead. Not everything that faces west is a sunset location.

Linger a while. I last came here on a frigid November afternoon when the gunmetal skies threatened an early snow. This was to be my last hiking day of the year before I yielded my beloved woods to my good friends, the hunters. Here I was, perched on a smallish boulder in a chill wind, looking upon fields that were lush just a couple of months ago. It was so brisk that even the usual complement of songbirds was not around to keep me company. It was me, a lone woodpecker, and a late-season red-tailed hawk working its way north around the ridge, losing its plaintive scream to an uncaring wind. Even in the monochrome brown of winter's first kiss, the frigid woods were a lovely place to be.

Reverse your route, head back to the car, and drive back to the entrance of the preserve.

There are two other worthy viewpoints along the paved road to the summit, East and West Views. East View is at GPS coordinates 39° 15.621′N, 77° 23.393′W, and West View, which is atop a stone building, is at GPS coordinates 39° 15.611′N, 77° 23.881′W. Both are nice. At East View, use the picnic table or rock pile as shooting perches. This view looks southeast onto handsome farmland dotted with upscale homes. An equipment shed on the left will be an issue.

At West View, don't bother with the view cutout; instead, climb the stairs to the top of a stone building near the parking area. Facing northwest, this high position puts you above the overgrowth that fouls the nearby view cutout. In the distance is Piner Rock and after that is South Mountain, home of the famed Appalachian Trail. Hidden in a notch on the view's left is Harpers Ferry.

Hike 39 Catoctin View, Frederick Municipal Forest, Frederick County

Catoctin View

Type: ledge	**Height:** 1,423 feet
Rating: 5	**Best time:** sunrise through midmorning
GPS, parking: 39° 34.108'N, 77° 27.406'W	**Difficulty:** easy
GPS, vista: 39° 34.143'N, 77° 27.186'W	**Distance:** .64 miles
Faces: 120°	**Time:** 35 minutes
Field of view: 60° to 140°	**Elevation change:** 126 feet
Relief: 40 feet	**Best lenses:** 35mm to 210mm
Elevation difference: 1,303 feet	

Directions: From Thurmont at the interchange of US-15 and MD-77, take MD-77 west toward Cunningham Falls and Catoctin Mountain Park for 2.5 miles. Turn left at the sign for Cunningham Falls and follow Catoctin Hollow Road uphill past the lake and out of the park for 2.9 miles, then turn left at a poorly signed T onto Mink Farm Road. Follow Mink Farm Road for 3.0 miles, then make a hard left at an acute angle onto Gambrill Park Road. You'll begin to climb a good-quality gravel road then descend again, following it for 3.0 miles and parking on the right in a large dirt pull off. Look for yellow gates off in the woods on both sides of the road. GPS coordinates: 39° 34.108'N, 77° 27.406'W.

This short trail leads to one stunner of a viewpoint. When I was scouting for this project, one of the maps I was using had a little vista symbol on it. Other symbols I had checked out didn't amount to much, so my success rate was not good and I didn't feel very efficient chasing all these unknowns. When I wandered out to Catoctin View, my jaw dropped. This is by far the absolute best east-facing viewpoint on the ridges of South and Catoctin Mountains. It is a must-do for everyone, whether a photographer or serious or casual hiker.

From the parking area, cross the gravel road, go around a gate, and follow a wide gravel path in a northeasterly direction, now on the blue-blazed Catoctin Trail. In .11 miles, arrive at clearing where three trails merge. Take the middle fork, blazed blue, which descends a few feet of flat rocks placed

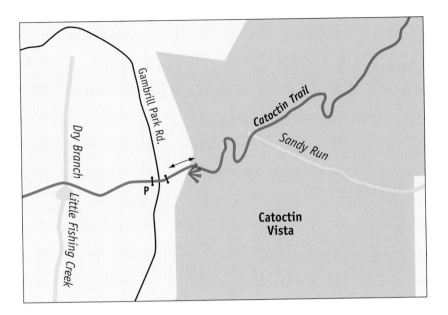

Catoctin View. I had shot a wide-pan sequence but Photoshop failed to stitch it properly. Turns out that featureless fog had no information for the merge routine to use. Thankfully, I had a backup plan by going graphic with a long lens. *Canon EOS 5D Mkii, Tokina 200-400, ISO100 setting, f16 @ .5s*

as pavers. Quickly, the trail becomes a woodland footpath and shortly after arrives at a view cutout and rock outcrop at .34 miles. This is the bucolic view I promised. Pretty sweet, isn't it?

Facing northeast, you'll be able shoot the summer solstice sunrise. Just out of view to the north (left) is Thurmont and, while audible, US-15 is also out of view far below. I came here a couple of times to shoot and every experience was different. However, I think the view works best when there's some ground fog so that the little ridges in the distance seem to poke through it. New snow would be better yet. I did have one serious problem in shooting a panoramic. Using a longer focal length to crop out the foreground brush left Photoshop with no clear edges to stitch the frames together. I ended up with a super-compressed product, and when I used the manual option two of the dozen frames flipped upside down. I never did get it to work quite the way I wanted it to, which was very frustrating. Moral of the story: include some foreground, then crop later.

Hike 40 Bob's Hill, Cunningham Falls State Park, Frederick County

Bob's Hill South

Type: ledge	**Field of view:** 126° to 178°
Rating: 3	**Relief:** 20 feet
GPS, parking: 39° 36.992'N, 77° 28.275'W	**Elevation difference:** 1,324 feet
GPS, vista: 39° 35.707'N, 77° 27.320'W	**Height:** 1,700 feet
Faces: 157°	**Best time:** sunrise through midmorning

Bob's Hill North

Type: ledge	**Relief:** 20 feet
Rating: 2	**Elevation difference:** 1,324 feet
GPS, vista: 39° 35.788'N, 77° 27.287'W	**Height:** 1,700 feet
Faces: 120°	**Best time:** sunrise through midmorning
Field of view: 110° to 160°	
Difficulty: moderate	**Elevation change:** 720 feet
Distance: 5.4 miles	**Best lenses:** 35mm to 210mm
Time: 3 hours, 15 minutes	

Directions: From Thurmont at the interchange of US-15 and MD-77, take MD-77 west toward Cunningham Falls and Catoctin Mountain Park for 2.5 miles and turn left at the sign for Cunningham Falls. Follow Catoctin Hollow Road uphill past the lake for 1.6 miles and park on the right in a wide area where a blue-blazed trail crosses the road (.3 miles after the signage for the falls and camp-ground that went right). GPS coordinates 39° 36.992'N, 77° 28.275'W.

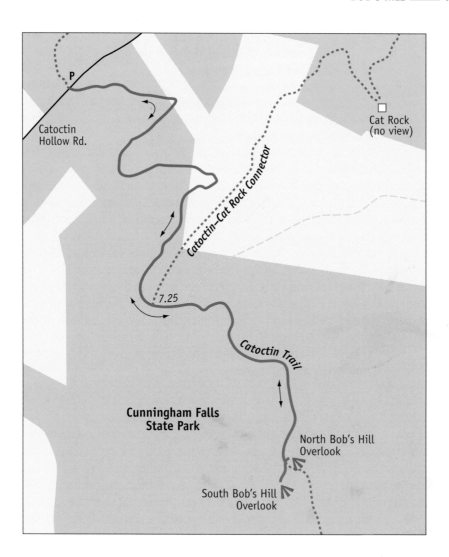

E ven if there wasn't a view at the end of this hike, it would still be worth your time to escape the crowds at Cunningham Falls and Catoctin; this section of the Catoctin Trail, although well blazed, gets very little use. This is unfortunate since the flat plateau atop Catoctin Mountain is some easy hiking through quiet woods.

Head uphill away from the parking area on the blue-blazed Catoctin trail. Blazes will be either dark or light blue rectangles with the occasional triangle or round one thrown in to keep you thinking. The trail's pitch is quite comfortable, although the long, broad switchbacks spend most of their time traversing a wide rock stream. The pitch slackens at .72 miles, and around .9 miles you gain the ridge top as you pass through a grove of mountain laurel. The trail is wide and you can set a brisk pace but you'll have to slow at 1.5 miles when you hit a rocky section.

Arrive at the well-signed, yellow-blazed trail for Cat Rock at 1.9 miles (39° 36.277'N, 77° 27.899'W). Continue ahead on the blue-blazed Catoctin Trail, which is wide, pretty level, with a nice leaves-off view to your left. When the trail narrows and becomes rockier near 2.5 miles, you're getting close to the crossing access trail for Bob's Hill, which you'll hit at 2.6 miles. Look for a 6x6 post on the left. If you find yourself pitching off the ridge and descending steeply through rock scree, you missed this.

Head left for Bob's Hill North, which is the lesser of the two views, and shortly come to some upturned ledges tucked in the tree line. This view is narrower than the southern one and faces southeast. Scan the horizon around 160° for a lone tower way off in the distance—to the naked eye it'll be as thin as a hair. This is the Washington Monument, sitting 53.7 miles away. You do need good, clear air for this.

Head back to the blue-blazed trail and cross it for South Bob's Hill. The narrow rocky trail runs about 40 yards or so to a larger and much flatter series of ledges that stand slightly above the surrounding trees. There are two distinct ledges. The left one has a view spanning 50°, looking southeast, and the right set of ledges has a much wider field of 142°, if you include the trees along the ridge surrounding the view. As with any mountain vista, fall color works best, although in morning light the closer trees will be side-lit enough to make any clear day workable. You can also see the monument from here.

Return to your car by reversing your route, arriving at 5.4 miles. However, if you'd like to make a side trip to the viewless Cat Rock (39° 36.965'N, 77° 26.944'W), feel free to do so. Head right at the signed yellow blaze, which you'll hit at 3.5 miles into your hike. Your total mileage if you include Cat Rock will be 9.25 miles, and you'll add another 200 feet of elevation gain. Also, at around the 5.5 mile mark, you'll encounter a red-blazed trail (39° 37.109'N, 77° 27.147'W) that doesn't appear park map so take your time, carefully compare the terrain to the map, and keep with the yellow-blazed trail.

Hike 41 Cunningham Falls, Cunningham Falls State Park, Frederick County

Type: slide	**Difficulty:** easy
Rating: 4	**Distance:** 1 mile
GPS: 39° 37.895'N, 77° 28.253'W	**Time:** 30 minutes
Stream: Big Hunting Creek	**Elevation change:** 100 feet
Height: 78 Feet	**Best lenses:** 17mm to 70mm
Best time: any time	

Directions: See page 108. Follow Catoctin Hollow Road uphill for 1.3 miles and turn right just after passing the lake. (Look for a sign for the falls and campground.) Follow the park road past the campground turnoff (on the left) for .7 miles and park in a large parking area for the lake and falls. GPS coordinates: 39° 37.666'N, 77° 27.859'W. NOTE—there is handicap-only parking area along MD-77 within sight of the falls.

Cunningham Falls is the highest fall in the state, locally very popular, relatively easy to get to, and located within easy driving distance of Baltimore and Washington. The punch line? Crowds, especially during fall color. Even so, on mid-week mornings and rainy days, it will pretty much be deserted.

From the large parking area, head up a flight of stairs back toward the road you entered on and come shortly to another parking area (which is

Cunningham Falls. Two images are stitched to create this shot, which wasn't my intention. I had shot the fall in three different positions in the frame, and when I got to post-processing none of them looked very good. Stitching them together gave me what I wanted—an environmental shot of the fall. *Canon EOS 5D Mkii, Canon 20-105L, polarizer, ISO100 setting, f16 @ 1s*

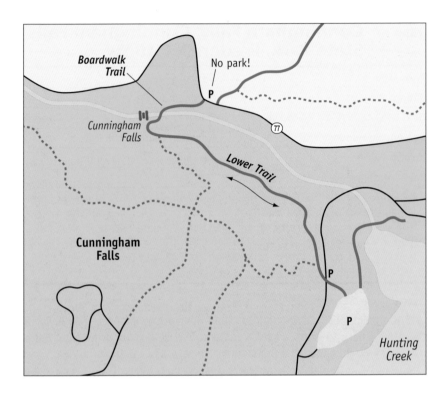

smaller and more crowded). Now, follow the red-blazed lower trail all the way to the falls. The wide gravel trail has a few ups and downs with one steep pitch near the beginning. It's a very pleasant walk. About halfway, look for some signage on the left facing the large boulder fall or rock stream that encroaches on the trail.

This is Catoctin metabasalt, one of the harder metamorphic rocks around. The lush green rocks actually have a greenish interior, which you'll see once you arrive at the exposed face of the fall's long slide. These rocks began as lava flows 600 million years ago, which were then buried at great depth where heat and pressure changed the crystal structure of the lava (metamorphosed) into a harder material. After millions of years of uplift and weathering, they're now back at the surface for you to enjoy.

Continue on to the falls. The view platform at the trail's end is not the best place to work from; instead, work from the rocks that extend into the small creek. The fall is a series of S-curves sliding around some choke stones. I think it's impossible to get an image of the entire water course. However, that's not an issue here since careful composition will create the illusion of continuous flow. There's one comfortable boulder on the left, and another good spot near the tree island on the right. It's an easy rock hop to get to the fall's foot, but take care! The plunge pool to the left is very deep and a popular swimming hole. It's best to shimmy up the ledges to your right and ever so carefully work from a small knob about 8 feet up.

Vegetation up the hillside can look scraggly in the fall, and the expanse of exposed rock on the right can be easily over-exposed. Sound like a challenge? Of all the falls I've shot—several hundred—this one has been the most challenging.

Don't forget to head downstream and look for interesting rock patterns to shoot. Also, the creek above the falls along MD-77 is quite attractive and worth exploring. There are several small pull-offs used by fisherman that provide easy access to the creek. The same goes for downstream of Catoctin Hollow Road, which is also a wonderful place to throw on the chest waders and explore a classic mountain stream.

Hike 42 Chimney Rock, Catoctin Mountain Park, Frederick County

Thurmont Vista

Type: ridge	**Field of view:** 123° to 143°
Rating: 1	**Relief:** 10 feet
GPS, parking: 39° 38.840'N, 77° 26.649'W	**Elevation difference:** 1,000 feet
GPS, vista: 39° 38.734'N 77° 26.352'W	**Height:** 1,502 feet
Faces: 133°	**Best time:** any time

Chimney Rocks

Type: cliff	**Relief:** 40 feet
Rating: 3	**Elevation difference:** 730 feet
GPS, vista: 39° 37.739'N, 77° 25.988'W	**Height:** 1,393 feet
Faces: 245°	**Best time:** early morning or late afternoon to sunset
Field of view: 190° to 300°	
Difficulty: difficult	**Elevation change:** 785 feet
Distance: 4.4 miles	**Best lenses:** 35mm to 210mm
Time: 2 hours, 30 minutes	

Directions: From Thurmont at the interchange of US-15 and MD-77, take MD-77 west toward Cunningham Falls and Catoctin Mountain Park for 2.4 miles and turn right into Catoctin Mountain Park. Head uphill on Park Central Road for 1.0 mile and park in a large parking area on the right, signed for Thurmont Vista upper parking lot. GPS coordinates: 39° 38.840'N, 77° 26.649'W.

This hike seems longer than it really is, probably because you climb over 400 feet outbound and climb just under 400 feet on the return. I guess as Bill Cosby famously said, "it's uphill . . . both ways." Head for the signed trail at the lot's north end and follow the gravel path up a moderately steep slope for .4 miles to the once-outstanding view at Thurmont Vista. The only thing clearly visible here is the pale blue water tower in Thurmont about 2.0 miles away.

From Thurmont Vista, the trail is generally uphill with some undulations. Around 1.46 miles, a rock face or large series of ledges appears on the left through the trees; this is Wolf Rocks. To get on top of this fascinating out-

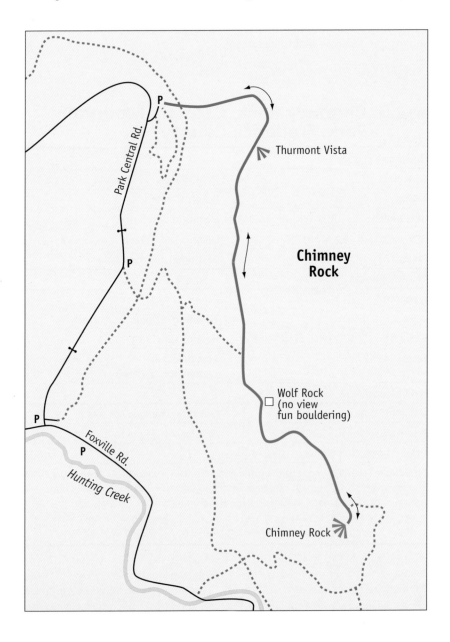

Chimney Rock. On a hot, overcast summer day, this is what you can expect. Unfortunately, Irene and Sandy ruined fall color shooting two years running. *Canon EOS 5D Mkii, Canon 20-105L, polarizer, ISO100 setting, f8 @ 1/20s*

crop, continue along the trail to 1.5 miles where you'll come to the second of two interpretive signs. From here, you can easily ascend the top of the dome. Wolf Rocks doesn't have a view; it's a unique geologic feature that provides a more intimate photographic experience. Look for patterns in the rock, lichen rings, tree roots, and other graphic forms. As you wander, take care with the fissures that split the dome in several places. Some are narrow, others quite wide, and all are very deep.

I encountered a large group of middle school and high school girls learning to rock climb. They were excited, boisterous, and chatty about how they were learning to tie knots, belay, find handholds, set cams, and all sorts of climbing skills. The rock dome is part of the Weverton Formation of sandstones, and here it caps a very hard rock formation called the greenstone. If you follow the slope of the dome, you'll see how it dips to the east. The dome's top is eroded away and Weverton outcrops appear on many of the ridges of Catoctin Mountain.

Head back to the interpretive sign and meander down the trail, keeping Wolf Rocks on your left. The formation eventually peters out and the trail becomes less used and more primitive. At 2.0 miles come to Chimney Rock, a fine southwesterly view overlooking MD-77 (which you can't see) and the flat top of Catoctin Mountain in Cunningham Falls State Park. There are several little outcrops that provide nice shooting perches. I prefer the ones on the view's right, which require you to hop over a 3-foot-wide by 20-foot-deep fissure to reach. There's a taller, free-standing pillar to the left but that's a little dicey to get to, even for me. In summer the surrounding green hills are muted because of haze, so I recommend spring and, of course, peak autumn color. I did look for snakes in all the little nooks and crannies and found none, not even any shed skins, so I'd say the outcrops are pretty much snake free.

As you came up MD-77, you made a pretty severe, climbing left-hand turn about halfway up from Thurmont Vista. If you looked to the right, you would have noticed how big boulders were choking the creek and extended up the steep slope out of sight. This is the rock stream that runs from Chimney Rock to the road. When you see it from the top end it doesn't look like much, but from below it looks pretty massive.

After you've hung out for a while, reverse your route and climb back toward Wolf Rocks, which will be on the right as you go by. Don't forget to hang a left and head downhill from Thurmont Vista to arrive at your car at 4.4 miles.

Hike 43 High Rock, Pen Mar Park, Washington County

High Rock

Type: cliff	Field of view: 228° to 352°
Rating: 5+	Relief: 100 feet
GPS, parking: 39° 41.704'N, 77° 31.423'W	Elevation difference: 1,000 feet
GPS, vista: 39° 41.704'N, 77° 31.423'W	Height: 1,834 feet
Faces: 290°	Best time: late afternoon to sunset

Pen Mar Pavilion

Type: ridge	Field of view: 250° to 010°
Rating: 4	Relief: 20 feet
GPS, parking: 39° 43.016'N, 77° 60.016'W	Elevation difference: 827 feet
GPS, vista: 39° 43.021'N, 77° 30.566'W	Height: 1,302 feet
Faces: 310°	Best time: morning or late afternoon
Difficulty: easy	Elevation change: none
Distance: 50 yards	Best lenses: 17mm to 400mm
Time: 10 minutes	

Directions: From Thurmont at the interchange of US-15 and MD-77, take US-15 north and exit onto MD-550 west for 9.3 miles, then turn right onto MD-550/491 at the entrance to Fort Ritchie. In .4 miles, turn left onto Pen Mar Road after crossing a railroad. In .2 miles, bear right after passing under the railroad to stay on Pen Mar Road. In another .2 miles continue to bear right, now on Buena Vista Road. Continue on Pen Mar Road for .7 miles; it will turn into Pen Mar High Rock Road near the entrance to Pen Mar Park. Stay on Pen Mar High Rock Road for 1.9 miles until the road ends at the view. Take care with the numerous speed humps, and be careful to not park anyone else in when you reach the end of the road. GPS coordinates: 39° 41.704'N, 77° 31.423'W.

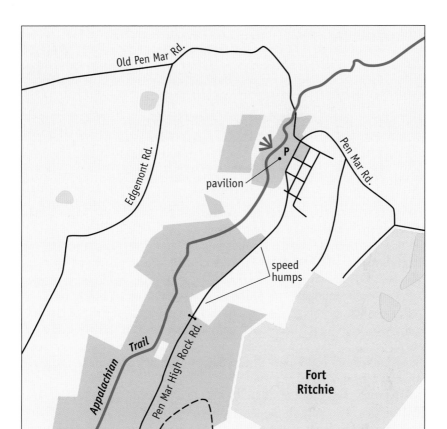

Old Pen Mar Rd.

Edgemont Rd.

Pen Mar Rd.

P

pavilion

speed
humps

Appalachian Trail

Pen Mar High Rock Rd.

Fort
Ritchie

towers
(federal)
no access

P

There are no superlatives: this is, hands-down, the best scenic view in all of Maryland. Just walk up the stairs and be amazed by what 1,000 feet of relief looks like. To the right is Waynesboro, Pennsylvania, and from there working left (south) there's nothing but farmland. This location is made for every lens you own, so shoot them all. When setting up at the view's precipice, take extra care with your tripod height. It may not be windy in the parking lot, but a few yards away in the open it's a different story. Don't forget that your camera strap will act like a sail. One issue with the view is that summer haze makes it difficult to shoot; spring and fall are much better. If

High Rock, Appalachian Trail. This pan sequence stitches together sixteen shots and at 2.3Gb spans almost 10 feet at full scale. High Rock is made for such techniques. *Canon EOS 5D Mkii, Canon 20-105L, 1 stop graduate, ISO100 setting, f16 @ 1/13s*

the road is closed due to snow you can park at the gate about .9 miles before the view and snowshoe in. (There's room for two or three cars.)

The view platform, which is a hang glider launch site, is a concrete slab that tilts toward the drop and overhangs the cliff face. It was closed for some time post 9/11 because to the southeast is Camp David and to the northeast is Raven Rock Mountain, site of the supposed "underground Pentagon." In doing research for this guide, I found that the site reopened in the last several years. Search for "High Rock hang gliding" in your browser or go to www.Hanggliding.org to see some cool videos. Unfortunately, I've missed every launching in the past three years, but that would make for some amazing photography.

As you head back out on High Rock Road, stop at the main parking area for Pen Mar Park, park in the large gravel lot to the right of the road, and walk over to the large picnic pavilion. This is also one heck of view and a nice quiet spot for lunch during the week. I've been here numerous times, and on every occasion I see a couple wander over, look out over the verdant

High Rock, Appalachian Trail. A simple telephoto shot of the farmland below this amazing viewpoint. I used a 200mm focal length to reach out and explore the graphic nature of the field boundaries. *Canon EOS 5D Mkii, Canon 70-200L, polarizer, ISO100 setting, f16 @ 1/13s*

valley, then turn and embrace. It has that kind of effect on people. In the right light, this would be a nice spot for wedding pictures, or better yet, an outdoor wedding. And since the famed Appalachian Trail runs past the pavilion, why not a 1,100-mile honeymoon backpack trip to Maine? Yeah, that's not happening.

Hike 44 Raven Rock and the Devil's Racecourse, Frederick County

Raven Rock

Type: cliff	Height: 1,353 feet
Rating: 2	Best time: any time
GPS, parking: 39° 39.876'N, 77° 32.176'W	Difficulty: moderate (to Raven Rock); easy (Devil's Racecourse)
GPS, vista: 39° 39.866'N, 77° 32.017'W	Distance: .6 miles (to Raven Rock; .4 miles (Devil's Racecourse)
Faces: 289°	Elevation change: 300 feet (to Raven Rock); 50 feet (Devil's Racecourse)
Field of view: 270° to 295°	Time: 30 minutes
Relief: 60 feet	Best lenses: 17mm to 135mm plus macro
Elevation difference: 654 feet	

Directions: To get to your first location, Raven Rock, from Thurmont at the interchange of US-15 and MD-77, take MD-77 west toward Cunningham Falls and Catoctin Mountain Park for 9.6 miles, passing both parks. At the traffic light for MD-64/Smithburg Pike, turn right onto MD-64 east. In .4 miles, turn right again onto Raven Rock Road. Take Raven Rock Road for 1.9 miles and when it makes a very long right to climb, look for guardrails on both sides and a yellow "45mph caution" sign. Park on either side at the downhill end of the guardrails—this is where the Appalachian Trail (AT) crosses. GPS coordinates: 39° 39.876'N, 77° 32.176'W.

    To get to The Devil's Racecourse from here, continue uphill on Raven Rock Road for another .3 miles (2.2 miles from MD-64) and make a hard left onto Ritchie Road. In .7 miles, park on the left at a small lane, easing to the right so you don't parked in. GPS coordinates: 39° 40.197'N, 77° 31.331'W.

These two short jaunts combine to make for a fun little tour of the two things that make the AT in Maryland and Pennsylvania famous—boulders and rocks. Or should that be rocks and boulders? Either way, you can have fun shooting a nifty little view and working your macro gear by shooting lichens and patterns.

To get to Raven Rock, face uphill on the road and turn left to head northbound on the AT. Climb quickly out of Raven Rock Hollow, working your way up a rock stream for .3 miles. On the right, you'll see a large rock outcrop and perhaps a poorly blue-blazed trail that heads to it from below. Look left and see where the AT climbs near a black rock face. Continue uphill for another several dozen yards until you're at the same height as the ledges. The AT switch-backs left—go right instead and head directly for the cliff. From here, scan the woods and see the blue blazes that were not visible from below.

It's a nice view looking west down Raven Rock Hollow. It may be a one-shot view, but the opportunity to shoot intimate scenes of Buzzard Knob across the hollow makes it worth the effort. I actually shot a series of panoramas whose increased aspect ratio worked better than the usual 4:3 horizontal. However, if you decide to shoot, keep the housing complex on the distant left out of view.

To return to your car, exit the view and head uphill a few yards, then go left to rejoin the AT. This is much easier than following the blue blazes down through a rock fall to join the AT below the view.

The Devil's Racecourse is super easy to reach. Head up the narrow rocky lane from the parking area, and after several yards in the trees pop out into a long, narrow rock stream. Turn right and rock hop uphill until you find a nice spot. The best lichen rings and rock tripe are on the left (west) side of the Racecourse, close to the trees. Look for upended rock slabs near some dead

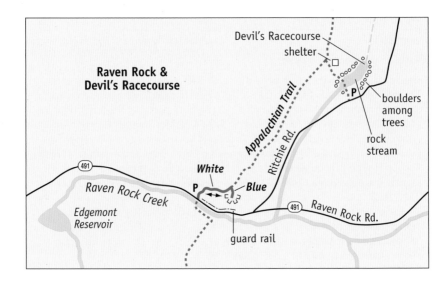

Raven Rock. This small ledge overhanging the forest below is meant for a wide angle. Unable to manage my foreground the way I had hoped, I went with a normal focal length and stitched three images together. Getting myself in the scene was not easy, even with a 15-second shutter delay. Note my left foot and you'll get sense of how uneven the ledge is. *Canon EOS 5D Mkii, Canon 20-105L, polarizer, ISO100 setting, f16 @ .5s*

Devil's Racecourse. Shot a couple dozen paces north of the blue blaze, this pan image stitches together ten images. The only way to show you how the rock stream felt was to use the widest image possible and to maximize depth of field with the widest lens I had, which is about 3 feet from the nearest boulder. *Canon EOS 5D Mkii, Tokina 17mm, ISO100 setting, f16 @ 1/6s*

trees. Besides the lichens, you can work overlapping rocks to create pleasing patterns. There is also the landscape of the rock stream. If you work farther uphill and look back, the woods surrounding the Racecourse doesn't look so healthy. However, when you're closer to the lane looking uphill the forest looks better, so I'd recommend that. I actually had some fun running the length of the Racecourse, although you can't move very quickly. It's more like a high-speed puzzle, the object of which is to not fall and break an arm.

Hike 45 Annapolis Rock, Washington County

Annapolis Rock

Type: cliff	Field of view: 196° to 274°
Rating: 5+	Relief: 80 feet
GPS, parking: 39° 32.127′N, 77° 36.259′W	Elevation difference: 1,265 feet
GPS, vista: 39° 33.455′N, 77° 35.931′W	Height: 1,762 feet
Faces: 235°	Best time: late afternoon to sunset

Black Rock

Type: cliff	Relief: 40 feet
Rating: 5+	Elevation difference: 1,400 feet
GPS, vista: 39° 34.367′N, 77° 35.800′W	Height: 1,800 feet
Faces: 235°	Best time: late afternoon to sunset
Field of view: 222° to 302°	
Difficulty: moderate to difficult	Elevation change: 840 feet
Distance: 7.4 miles	Best lenses: 17mm to 400mm
Time: 3 hours, 30 minutes	

Directions: From I-70 exit 42, take MD-17 north for .5 miles and turn right onto Ellerton Road at a white brick building that looks like an old bank. In .4 miles go left onto US-40 west and in 3.0 miles *carefully* bear left at the top of a rise into wide parking area. Eastbound traffic crests the hill on a somewhat blind turn. GPS coordinates: 39° 32.127′N, 77° 36.259′W.

This is a really fun hike to two of the best views in all of Maryland. At the west end of the lot is a large sign and berm that keeps cars off old US-40. There'll be some signage marking the trailhead. The lot fills quickly anytime the weather is nice and can be really tight by 8:00 A.M. on weekends. In the summer, look for a couple of fruit vendors a little east of the lot.

Follow the large blue arrow, walk along the old paved road, and bear left at a blue blaze to arrive at the white-blazed Appalachian Trail (AT) after about 100 yards. The AT ahead crosses I-70 on a footbridge to head southbound for Washington Monument State Park and Georgia. Go right to head northbound for Annapolis Rock. I-70 will be on your left and you'll pass under US-40.

The trail is a cobble-filled woods road that climbs steadily for 460 feet, but not so abruptly as to be unenjoyable, and summits Pine Knob at .86 miles. Now it descends, slowly losing about 200 feet before bottoming out at 1.11 miles. From here to the blue-blazed trail to Annapolis Rock, the AT is a wide woods road with a gentle, undulating uphill grade. You can certainly set a fast pace, but why bother unless you're running late for sunset?

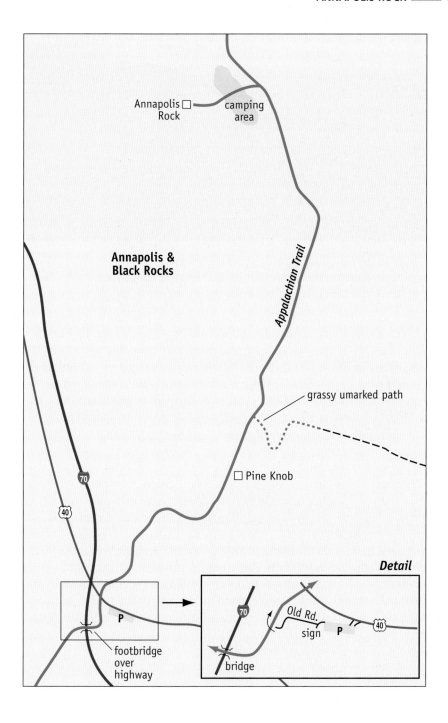

Annapolis Rock

camping area

Annapolis & Black Rocks

Appalachian Trail

grassy umarked path

☐ Pine Knob

70

40

P

footbridge over highway

Detail

70

Old Rd. sign

P

40

bridge

Annapolis Rock. This location is built for panoramic shooting. Having shot many sequences, I settled on this twilight shot because the cliffs picked out the pastel hues of the sky. A little post-process work was done to remove the flood lights from the drag strip near the center. *Canon EOS 5D Mkii, Canon 20-105L, 2 stop graduate, ISO100 setting, f8 @ .5s*

At 2.31 miles come to the blue-blazed trail that goes left for the view; it's a little under a quarter mile of rocky trail that descends slightly to the extensive cliffs of Annapolis Rock. Pass through a campground and a semi-permanent camp for the campground steward, who's employed by the Potomac Appalachian Trail Club. Arrive at the view at 2.54 miles.

There are three large promontories that encompass the view. The southern (leftmost) will be the loneliest when it comes time to shoot. The largest platform is the central one—the rock shelf at the view's rear makes for natural amphitheater seating, but if you set up here you may be asked to move since you'll be in the way of up to a hundred people. The northern (rightmost) ledge is higher than the others and will have other photographers camped out in their spots over an hour before sunset. This is why the southernmost ledges are the best.

I spent some time talking to the PATC steward, and she was a very interesting person with a really cool summer job. Imagine getting paid to camp out for a couple months on the AT. I was camping at Cunningham Falls State Park and rode out a scary thunderstorm the evening before I made my scouting hike to Annapolis Rock. There was a Girl Scout troop rock climbing and camping at Annapolis Rock that night. The storm blew off my rain fly and left a number of other campers screaming in the bathrooms. It was one of the more violent storms I've ever been through. The scouts hunkered down in their tents and came through it fine. When I asked them how it was, the group was rather upbeat, with one girl saying how "totally cool" it was. Not sure if I would have had the same enthusiastic critique.

After you've filled a memory card or two, head back up the blue-blazed trail to the AT and at 2.77 miles go left (northbound) and head along a level trail section and toward Black Rock. As you move along, you'll notice views through the trees to your left. Don't bother bushwhacking any of these, as they're tree-filled cobbles surrounding Annapolis Rock. Around 3.1 miles the AT attains a small rise and swings left (west) to head to the ridge flank. You'll come parallel to the ridge's edge at 3.31 miles and as you move along a level section, rocks begin to appear on the left. At 3.65 miles, come to an unsigned and un-blazed but well-used path on the left. Go left to another stunner of a view.

The view extends several degrees north of 300° but a group of dead trees mars that side of the view, which is why I have the view's field listed as such. The rock slabs you're on have numerous potholes which, when filled with water, will make unique foregrounds. Black Rock takes its name from the extensive black lichen cover which has been pretty much worn off. The cobble below the view is huge and what you see, if only the southern end, extends a good quarter mile north. There is an east-facing exposure farther north, which I had been told was also incredible, but it's overgrown.

Reverse your route and remember to not cross the footbridge over I-70. Do some business with the fruit vendors if any are around.

Hike 46 Washington Monument State Park, Washington County

Monument Knob

Type: ridge	Height: 1,540 feet
Rating: 3	Best time: any time
GPS, parking: 39° 29.954'N, 77° 37.528'W	Difficulty: easy
GPS, vista: 39° 30.025'N, 77° 37.415'W	Trail: .6 miles
Faces: 304°	Time: 30 minutes
Field of view: 278° to 330°	Elevation change: 80 feet
Relief: 10 feet	Best lenses: 17mm to 400mm
Elevation difference: 950 feet	

Directions: From I-70 exit 42, take MD-17 north .8 miles and turn left onto Washington Monument Road to head west. Take Washington Monument Road for 1.1 miles, then turn right onto a wider version of Washington Monument Road. In .7 miles, Washington Monument Road goes left again to go under I-70. In 2.0 miles turn right into Washington Monument Rock State Park and climb the steep and narrow park road to park in one of the large lots near the park office/museum. GPS coordinates: 39° 29.954'N, 77° 37.528'W.

Find the white-blazed Appalachian Trail (AT), uphill from the museum near a stone wall, and follow it northbound (uphill). There will be a sign for the monument. The wide gravel trail cuts left at .22 miles where the AT goes right to head to Maine. Arrive at the monument at .3 miles.

Washington Monument Rock. This is the northwest-facing view from the tower's top. The boulder field below spans about 3 acres and in summer just radiates heat if you venture into it. *Canon EOS 5D Mkii, Canon 20-105L, 1 stop graduate, ISO100 setting, f8 @ 1/60s*

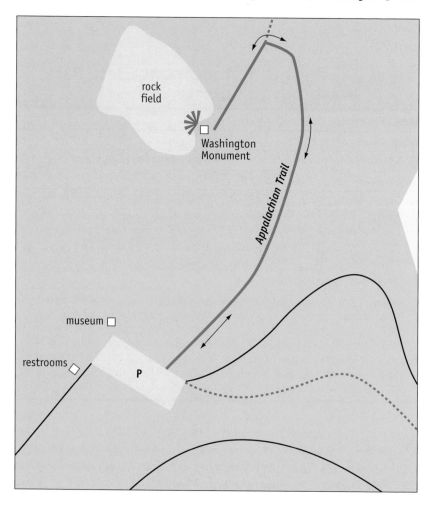

The view northwest from the tower's base is impressive although the valley around Boonsboro is fairly built up. This is the only reason this is a 3 for an otherwise lovely view. The tower is open for climbing and the view is even better from here, and much wider. Three distinct sightlines provide the best shooting: west along 262°, northwest along 345°, and southeast along 126°. It's a quick out-and-back that certainly doesn't take much time, but that doesn't mean it's not worth your time—it is. If the road is closed due to snow, or some other reason, park along Monument Road just north of the entrance and hike the AT up the monument. It'll be a little over .5 miles, with a 300-foot climb. You can imagine what the view would be like with a fresh blanket of snow during the glow of dawn.

Hike 47 Weverton Cliffs, Washington County

Type: cliff	Height: 656 feet
Rating: 5	Best time: sunrise through late morning, late afternoon through sunset
GPS, parking: 39° 19.983'N, 77° 41.013'W	Difficulty: difficult
GPS, vista: 39° 19.929'N, 77° 40.604'W	Distance: 1.6 miles
Faces: 230°	Time: 1 hour
Field of view: 180° to 288°	Elevation change: 675 feet
Relief: 60 feet	Best lenses: 17mm to 200mm
Elevation difference: 430 feet	

Directions: From US-340 and MD-17 near Brunswick, take US-340 west for 2.6 miles and exit onto MD-67 toward Boonsboro. Make the first right onto Rohrersville/Weverton Road. In about .1 miles, park on the right in the large "Park and Ride" lot. GPS coordinates: 39° 19.983'N, 77° 41.013'W.

Exit the parking area and turn right onto Weverton Road, where you'll see a white blaze on the guard rail. Head for the T-intersection ahead where Weverton Road heads steeply uphill and a dead end is downhill. The white-blazed Appalachian Trail will appear as a gap in the brush on the hillside in front of you.

An apparently never-ending series of switchbacks provides a delightfully intense hike up the side of South Mountain. At .5 miles come to a blue-blazed side trail that goes right to Weverton Cliffs; the AT continues uphill to the left. Having only made it up half the ridge's height, you'll now drop about 60 feet to the view, arriving at .8 miles. Weverton Cliffs is the tan, quartzite-based sandstone cap rock of the Weverton formation that forms this end of South Mountain. Farther north, the cap rock is the hard, white

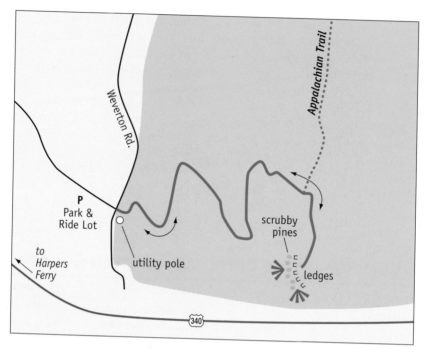

Weverton Cliff. A simple, handheld shot. Sometimes a tripod can be a burden to creativity, particularly on such uneven rock ledges. *Canon EOS 5D Mkii, Canon 20-105L, 1 stop graduate, ISO100 setting, f8 @ 1/30s*

Weverton Cliff. On a day the sky had started to glow an epic pastel pink, the cloud deck quickly covered the sun. Even so, this predawn image has some interesting character to it, although it's certainly no knockout. Note the headlamp streaks, the train locomotive, and the glow of Harpers Ferry beyond. *Canon EOS 5D Mkii, Canon 20-105L, 1 stop graduate, ISO100 setting, f8 @ 6s*

Tuscarora sandstone that is the hallmark of the Ridge and Valley provinces of Maryland and Pennsylvania.

The view is surrounded by pines. The best exposures require you to hang very close to the edges of the radically up-tilted sandstone fingers. Looking upstream along the Potomac, you'll note US-340 clearly cuts the scene from left to right; this is not a problem if you set your tripod low. Just be careful how you place your feet and those of your tripod, as it's a long way down. Sunrise will be behind you and light the valley long after Maryland Heights lights up, so a graduated filter is a must-have here. If you can get fog in the valley, capping the river, you'll have a great shot.

As I was parking my car well before dawn on a crisp autumn day, several cars pulled up and out hopped a crew of ultra-runners. Their plan was to carpool to Pen Mar Park on the Mason-Dixon Line and run the nearly 44 miles back to this point. They had a support vehicle with food and water that would meet this rather fit-looking cadre at various road crossings as they ran south. A few years ago, I would have looked upon them as being nearly insane. Now I am one of them, albeit a very slow member of their species. Don't knock it until you've tried it.

Hike 48　Maryland Heights, Washington County

Type: cliff	Height: 503 feet
Rating: 5+	Best time: sunrise through late morning, late afternoon through sunset
GPS, parking: 39° 19.744'N, 77° 43.896'W	Difficulty: difficult
GPS, vista: 39° 19.490'N, 77° 43.552'W	Distance: 5.3 miles
Faces: 150°	Time: 4 hours
Field of view: 126° to 168°	Elevation change: 1,620 feet
Relief: 100 feet	Best lenses: 20mm to 200mm
Elevation difference: 263 feet	

Directions: From US-340 and MD-17 near Brunswick, take US-340 west for 3.6 miles and turn left onto Keep Tryst/Valley Road. The turn is just after the divided highway ends where US-340 curves south to cross the Potomac. In .2 miles turn right onto Sandy Hook Way. Follow Sandy Hook Way for 2.1 miles to one of three parking areas glued to the cliff face on the right. As you get close to the river, the road narrows and makes a little jog left before going under US-340. As you get close to the last house on the right, Sandy Hook Way makes a sudden left over a bridge to cross the railroad below. This little turn is a huge surprise and I almost got hit twice by inattentive drivers. GPS coordinates: 39° 19.744'N, 77° 43.896'W.

Parking will be at an extreme premium on weekends. The first parking area at the trailhead has room for about eight cars if they park door to door. About .1 miles farther on there is room for another sixteen cars, and where Sandy Hook Way turns right is room for another two. To get between parking areas, use the canal tow path and footbridges. Don't walk along the narrow Sandy Hook Way.

Head up the steep rocky road and at .18 miles arrive at the first of many signs that give you an excuse to stop and rest. As you climb, the trail swings right at .34 miles to follow a handsome stream that sits down a steep slope on the left. If conditions for vista shooting aren't all that good, you could pitch off the trail and scramble down to work this little stream.

Pass under a pole line at .45 miles and see your return route come in from the left at .55 miles. Next, come to the "Naval Battery" at .67 miles. There's no view from here but a quick loop around the battery is fairly interesting. The effort to haul heavy cannon up this ridge is mind-boggling. At .76 miles, the second part of the green-blazed loop out to the stone fort (which runs the ridge's west side) comes in on your left. Instead, go straight on the now red-blazed trail and continue climbing, then at 1.0 mile join the blue-blazed trail, which is the portion of the stone fort loop on the east side of the ridge. You're now at the first high point of your hike. Be prepared to lose 405 feet

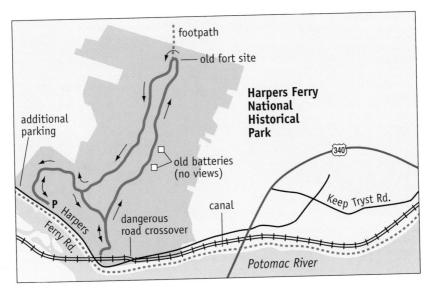

footpath

old fort site

**Harpers Ferry
National
Historical
Park**

additional
parking

old batteries
(no views)

340

Keep Tryst Rd.

P Harpers

Ferry Rd.

dangerous
road crossover

canal

Potomac River

in just less than .5 miles. Continue ahead on the red-blazed trail to the view, arriving at 1.4 miles.

Spectacular, isn't it? It was a lot of work but it's certainly worth it. The cliffs are triangular with pinnacles at several different heights. I think the best spot is to the left of the large fissure that divides the view into two distinct sections—the right section looks up the Potomac and the left section looks more upon Harpers Ferry and Shenandoah River. Explore each of the dozen or so little perches and absorb the view. Don't try to get to the lone free-standing pillar near the large fissure—it's a very long way down.

It was about 95° with a heat index over 100° when I got here around 1:00 P.M., precisely the time of day when you don't want to be exerting yourself by climbing up a steep trail. I was glad I had decided put hydration salts in my camel pack and to bring extra water just in case. I was

Maryland Heights. The only way to get this self portrait was to give my camera to somebody else. They were very nervous about holding such a big camera, but I reassured them by saying, "if you hear a scream and then the viewfinder is empty, it's yours." That didn't quite reassure them. *Canon EOS 5D Mkii, Canon 20-105L, 1 stop graduate, ISO100 setting, f6 @ 1/100s*

Maryland Heights. A handheld pan shows both the cliffs and the view at the same time. You can easily see why this made an impressive artillery battery. Note the canal path and road below the cliffs. *Canon EOS 5D Mkii, Canon 20-105L, 1 stop graduate, ISO100 setting, f8 @ 1/25s*

hanging out, jotting notes and making compass measurements, when a young couple showed up and sat nearby. They had emptied their two 16-ounce water bottles. I overheard the young lady complaining of a persistent headache and a cramp in one calf. This was not good. Cramping, and worse yet a headache, are sure signs of potentially dangerous heat stress. I offered them some food and water, but they politely refused. It was at this point that I firmly said: "Young lady, you have a serious problem. You'll drink and eat what's offered or you're not going to make it back to your car." They both looked at me, then finally accepted the bag of nuts I handed them as I filled their water bottles from my pack's bladder. The point of this is simple: don't mess around with the heat. Bring ample water and salty snacks and consume both as needed. (I had about 100 ounces of water with me). When it comes to proper hydration, here's a good rule of thumb: if you don't feel like you can pee, then you've got a problem. Also, take your time. You won't be able to pound up a hill like this when it's 100° the same way you can when it's 70°. Be smart and listen to your body. The young lady's headache subsided and her cramping ceased after about twenty minutes.

After climbing back to the blue-blazed trail junction, turn right, and continue climbing up a nearly stairway-steep section before topping out at 1.75 miles. Pass the powder magazine at 2.2 miles. Now on the level, you'll pass large rocks and ledges on the right at 2.4 miles, where there's a leaves-off view. About .25 miles farther along, come to another viewpoint that's a narrow alley through the trees and looks down on the Potomac. This is the 100-pound battery, the weight referring to the size of the ball fired. The guns weighed many tens of tons, and I'm still in awe of how they got them up here.

Arrive at the remains of the stone fort at 3.0 miles. The trail now goes left through the fort to head you back south along the ridge's west side. There's a brown National Park directional sign to guide the way. An un-blazed trail

continues along Elk Ridge for several miles to some rocky outcrops that don't provide a view. Continue the long looping left and descend some stairs past the fort's exterior to head southbound along the ridge, now parallel to your northbound path. Above you to the left are exposed rocks and ledges, which will remain with you until about 3.5 miles.

The trail has a gradual descent until it makes a serious pitch off the ridge to rejoin the green-blazed trail (your initial uphill route) at 3.9 miles. Turn right and head back to your car, arriving at 5.3 miles. It's a nice hike, and although it's very steep in places, the views were more than worth it.

Hike 49 Log Roll Overlook, Green Ridge State Forest, Allegany County

Type: Ridge	**Elevation difference:** 600 feet
Rating: 5+	**Height:** 1,276 feet
GPS, parking: 39° 34.499'N, 78° 30.763'W	**Best time:** late afternoon though sunset and twilight
GPS, vista: 39° 34.499'N, 78° 30.763'W	**Difficulty:** easy
Faces: 291°	**Distance:** 10 yards
Field of view: 254° to 328°	**Elevation change:** none
Relief: 10 feet	**Best lenses:** 28mm to 200mm

Directions: From I-68 exit 62 for Fifteen Mile Creek, take the paved Fifteen Mile Creek Road south away from the interstate. As soon as you pass the youth services center, follow the now gravel road for 2.0 miles. You'll cross Fifteen Mile Creek, then begin to climb steeply on a well-rutted road section. As you top out near the 2-mile mark you'll bear right at a Y onto the much smoother Green Ridge Road. Follow Green Ridge Road for 6.4 miles and park on the right at a picnic area near Kirk Road. GPS coordinates: 39° 34.499'N, 78° 30.763'W.

Walk through a gap in the fence and go about 10 yards to this excellent viewpoint of a meander in Hides Run. To get the best image, move to the left and drag the picnic table with you to gain a little extra relief.

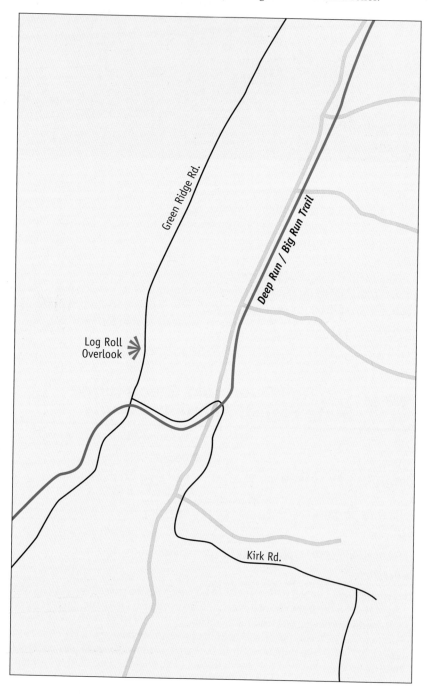

Log Roll Vista. Shot in morning light, this image had a huge contrast problem, even with proper filtration technique. Although I'm not fond of the process, I did an HDR of three images. *Canon EOS 5D Mkii, Canon 20-105L, 1 stop graduate, ISO100 setting, f22 @ 1/4s*

Log Roll Vista. What a wonderful evening to make photographs. This is the kind of sky photographers live for. *Canon EOS 5D Mkii, Canon 20-105L, 1 stop graduate, ISO100 setting, f16 @ 4s*

Hike 50 Banner's Overlook, Allegany County

Type: ridge	**Elevation difference:** 1,190 feet
Rating: 5+	**Height:** 1,657 feet
GPS, parking: 39° 35.726'N, 78° 28.700'W	**Best time:** morning twilight through sunrise
GPS, vista: 39° 35.726'N, 78° 28.700'W	**Difficulty:** easy
Faces: 120°	**Distance:** 80 yards
Field of view: 80° to 160°	**Elev. Change:** None
Relief: 20 feet	**Gear:** 28mm to 200mm

Directions: See page 133. Follow Green Ridge Road for 4.2 miles and turn left onto the coarse gravel of Mertens Avenue. You'll drop quickly, cross Deep Creek, and then climb steeply again, hitting one rather tight switchback. After 1.9 miles you'll top out and turn right into a large parking lot signed for Stafford Road ORV Trail. This trail is closed to all vehicles, and if you make the mistake anywhere in Green Ridge of turning onto Stafford Road, you're in for serious trouble unless you have a "rock crawling"–capable 4WD. GPS coordinates: 39° 35.726'N, 78° 28.700'W.

Walk through a gap in the fence and go about 40 yards to where the ridge drops away. "Wow" is a pretty good description for this location. Facing southeast, the view is dominated by two large trees that limit the field of view. Looking out over the heavily wooded West Virginia meander of the Potomac above Lock 61, you don't really have a view of the river. You do have a view of Sideling Hill 6.5 miles away in the middle distance and Cacapon Mountain farther out at 10 miles.

Banner Overlook. This eight-image pan required a little planning. The sun couldn't be in overlapping images, just centered in one, otherwise the lens flare wouldn't stitch properly. Neither could it be fully above the ridge for the same reason. So, I shot the sun-centered image first and then the rest as quickly as possible. *Canon EOS 5D Mkii, Canon 20-105L, 2 stop graduate, ISO100 setting, f8 @ 1/8s*

The foreground is just a bunch of messy grass, so a wide angle won't produce a very good shot; however, you can crop out what doesn't work. Don't forget to try shooting a pan or two.

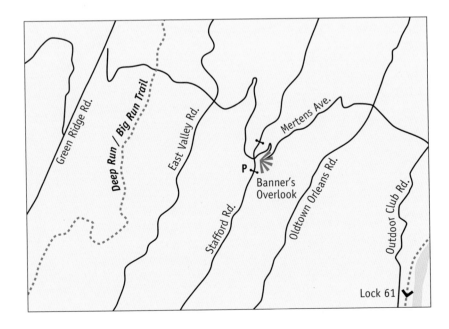

Hike 51 | No Name Vista, Garrett County

Type: ridge	**Height:** 1562 feet
Rating: 5+	**Best time:** sunrise through late morning, late afternoon through sunset
GPS, parking: 39° 38.933'N, 78° 26.693'W	**Difficulty:** difficult
GPS, vista: 39° 38.805'N, 78° 26.389'W	**Distance:** 1.4 miles
Faces: 150°	**Time:** 50 minutes
Field of view: 128° to 170°	**Elevation change:** 395 feet
Relief: 10 feet	**Best lenses:** 20mm to 200mm
Elevation difference: 600 feet	

Directions: From I-68 exit 62 for Fifteen Mile Creek, take the paved Fifteen Mile Creek Road south away from the interstate. As soon as you pass the youth services center, follow the now gravel road for 3.3 miles, passing Green Ridge Road. When you get to where Stafford Road T's to the right, bear right on Stafford Road for about .3 miles and park in a dirt lot. Ahead will be the closed Stafford Road ORV trail, and to the left a gated section of the closed Stafford Road. GPS coordinates: 39° 38.933'N, 78° 26.693'W.

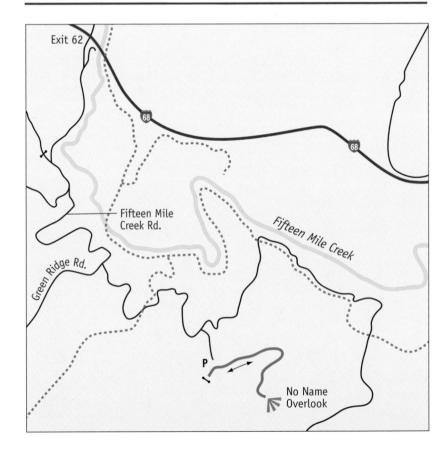

The Stafford Road ORV trail was closed permanently in 2011, and as you walk up the road you'll discover why. From the parking area, bear left onto the continuation of Stafford Road and follow it steeply uphill for .7 miles. As you climb the deeply rutted road, look right into the woods and notice how ORV owners have cut more challenging trails. This level of destruction is one reason why the entire ORV trail was closed. Now you can see why a wrong turn on Stafford Road at any point in Green Ridge would be a very bad idea.

When you come to a large parking area on the right at the mountain's crest, the view will be on the left. An old fence marks the view and a few yards beyond is an overgrown grassy opening. If you stand to the left of the large white oak, you'll be in the best spot. The next ridge beyond is Cacapon State Park in West Virginia. The view is not as nice as Point Overlook, or even Banner's Overlook, but it is still quite nice and worth the steep road march. Enjoy.

Hike 52 **Point Lookout, Allegany County**

Type: cliff	**Elevation difference:** 307 feet
Rating: 5+	**Height:** 769 feet
GPS, parking: 39° 37.477'N, 78° 26.060'W	**Best time:** sunrise through late morning
GPS, vista: 39° 37.462'N, 78° 26.040'W	**Difficulty:** easy
Faces: 150°	**Distance:** 60 yards
Field of view: 90° to 210°	**Elevation change:** 20 feet
Relief: 60 feet	**Best lenses:** 17mm to 200mm

Directions: It's only 8.2 miles from I-68 but this route is slow going due to all the switchbacks. From I-68 exit 62 for Fifteen Mile Creek, take the paved Fifteen Mile Creek Road south away from the interstate. As soon as you pass the youth services center follow the now gravel road for 3.3 miles, passing Green Ridge Road, and when you get to where Stafford Road T's to the right, go straight onto Dug Hill Road and drop once again to Fifteen Mile Creek. (As I said in Hike 51, Stafford is bad news.) You'll be on Dug Hill Road for a long, sometimes rough 3.9 miles before turning left onto the well-graded Oldtown Orleans Road. In .8 miles come to a Y and go right on Carroll Road for .2 miles. Park on the right in the large pull-off. GPS coordinates: 39° 35.477'N, 78° 26.060'W.

Yep, it was a long drive but it's a heck of a view! In fact, it's the best view in Green Ridge and well worth a predawn alarm to get here for sunrise. Cross Carroll Road, descend the stairs to the walled view, and enjoy. The best set-up is atop the wall, where you'll have just a bit more relief so that

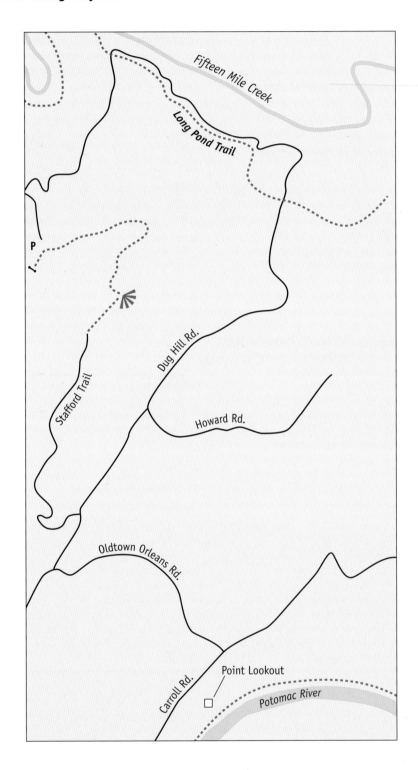

Point Overlook. I always envisioned this location as a panoramic. Standing atop the wall with my lens set at 20mm, I was able to capture the Potomac's full meander. The only way to avoid lens flare was to shoot before the sun came up. *Canon EOS 5D Mkii, Canon 20-105L, 2 stop graduate, ISO100 setting, f10 @ 1s*

foreground brush won't sneak into the frame. A small perch below the wall is pretty nice, too. Fall color is nice since the hill beyond is lush with woods; however, the trees on the lower left on this side of the river will drop their leaves way earlier than any others in the scene. Careful composition is a must. If you can get here in snow then please do—that will be the killer shot. This location is made for panoramic photography, so have fun!

Hike 53 **Bill Shipley Overlook, Allegany County**

Type: ledge	**Height:** 995 feet
Rating: 3	**Best time:** morning
GPS, parking: 39° 39.887'N, 78° 26.571'W	**Difficulty:** easy
GPS, vista: 39° 39.862'N, 78° 26.646'W	**Distance:** 100 yards
Faces: 215°	**Time:** 10 minutes
Field of view: 160° to 270°	**Elevation change:** 30 feet
Relief: 40 feet	**Best lenses:** 35mm to 200mm
Elevation difference: 320 feet	

Directions: From I-68 exit 64 for Green Ridge State Forest, take M.V. Smith Road south for about 100 yards and turn right onto Headquarters Drive. Park in the large parking loop near the forest office. GPS coordinates: 39° 39.887'N, 78° 26.571'W.

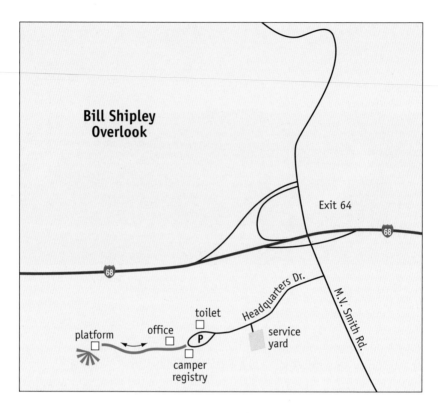

Bill Shipley Overlook

Follow the signed, paved, handicap-accessible pathway past the forest office to the large wooden view platform dedicated to Bill Shipley. This very well-maintained viewpoint looks down onto a tightly entrenched meander of Fifteen Mile Creek. To your left is the northern terminus of Town Hill where Stafford Vista is (Hike 51). This is a good fall color spot since the view is basically about a mile. Look for graphic patterns in the heavy tree cover on the surrounding ridge flanks.

Troutman Road, Allegany County

Polish Mountain Vista

Type: ridge	**Height:** 1,389 feet
Rating: 5	**Best time:** afternoon through sunset and twilight
GPS, parking: 39° 40.944'N, 78° 32.004'W	**Difficulty:** easy
GPS, vista: 39° 40.942'N, 78° 32.047'W	**Distance:** .3 miles
Faces: 280°	**Time:** 25 minutes
Field of view: 240° to 320°	**Elevation change:** 70 feet
Relief: 10 feet	**Best lenses:** 35mm to 200mm
Elevation difference: 650 feet	

Directions: From I-68 exit 62 for Fifteen Mile Creek, take MD-144/National Pike west for 3.8 miles and make a hard left onto Gilpin Road, then in .3 miles turn off the pavement onto the gravel Troutman Road and climb. In .9 miles, park on the left opposite a yellow gate where the purple-blazed bike trail crosses the road. GPS coordinates: 39° 40.944'N, 78° 32.004'W.

This short hike to a clear view cutout on the flank of Polish Mountain brings you to an excellent sunset location. The view cutout is full of slash, and it can be a bit of a challenge to find comfortable footing once you're into it. If you're here in damp, humid conditions, this may be a good time to bring a head net—the gnats can be very persistent. However, it's really a fall color shot, so bugs shouldn't be an issue then.

Walk past the gate and in a few yards cross the Great Eastern Trail and bike path which is blazed purple inside of white. Walk another 50 yards along a grass woods road to an obvious ATV trail and go left over a little berm. (The grass woods road continues straight.) The path you're now on

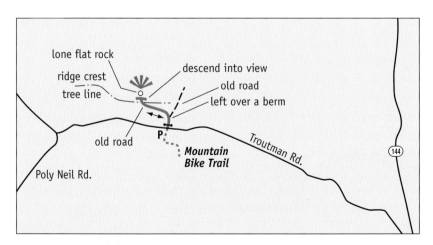

Troutman Road Vista. In this twelve-image pan, the sun could only appear in one frame, otherwise lens flare would be a serious problem, as it would have been with the sun above the ridge. By shooting the sun first and centered in the frame, I was able to eliminate this problem. *Canon EOS 5D Mkii, Canon 20-105L, 2 stop graduate, ISO100 setting, f8 @ 1/6s*

leads directly to the view, but it has one trick—the ATV path peters out quickly to become an ancient road depression, and a couple blowdowns conspire with a raspberry bramble to force you off course. Just head the short .1 miles toward an obvious gap in the trees ahead.

The view is in need of some thinning out; however, there are some good spots about 20 yards down-slope near two large tree stumps, and an exposed rock slab provides a nice flat spot from which to work. From here the view is wide and the valley of Town Creek below is quite pleasant. Tom Hill is the near ridge slightly left of center, 2.75 miles away. The farthest ridge in sight, just right of center, is Evitts Mountain at Rocky Gap State Park, 8 miles out. On my third trip to shoot sunset, the wind was from the left and it carried the road noise of I-68 away from me. It was such a delightful evening and I hung out well past sunset just to listen for owls. My dinner of granola bars was rather tasty in the chilly twilight.

Hike 55 Canyon Overlook, Rocky Gap State Park, Allegany County

Type: cliff	**Height:** 1,219 feet
Rating: 4	**Best time:** midmorning through late afternoon
GPS, parking: 39° 41.760'N, 78° 39.861'W	**Difficulty:** easy
GPS, vista: 39° 41.876'N, 78° 39.994'W	**Distance:** .33 miles
Faces: 304°	**Time:** 20 minutes
Field of view: 274° to 330°	**Elevation change:** 70 feet
Relief: 80 feet	**Best lenses:** 20mm to 200mm
Elevation difference: 138 feet	

Directions: From I-68 exit 50 for Rocky Gap State Park, enter the park and turn left for the lodge and golf course parking/bag drop. Take the road for .8 miles to where it ends at a parking lot for Canyon Overlook Nature Trail and the aviary. GPS coordinates: 39° 41.760'N, 78° 39.861'W.

From the car, head up the paved road and pass a large gate with a sign that says "Pedestrians and Bike Only." The aviary will be on the right. In about 60 yards turn left up a few stairs and take the left fork of the nature loop. Arrive at the view in .19 miles. If you look down the gap at the left ridge, you'll see cliffs near the top—that's your next spot.

The view is restricted by the pines growing from the rock face. To get the best shot to the left, set up near the tree on the right, and vice versa. Out of sight but still audible is Rocky Gap Run, which snakes through the gap from your right to left. The gap itself is an ancient fault line that slices through the end of Evitts Mountain; this explains why the run follows this route instead of an easier path. As with other tight locations, fall color would be best but a nice snow scene would be even better.

Head back to your car, returning at .33 miles, and zero out your GPS before heading to the next view, Hike 56.

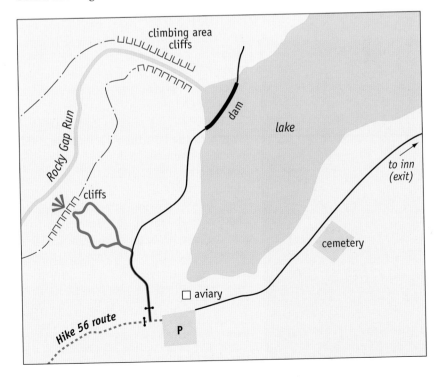

Hike 56 Rocky Gap, Rocky Gap State Park, Allegany County

Type: cliff	Height: 1,334 feet
Rating: 4	Best time: midmorning through late afternoon
GPS, parking: 39° 41.760'N, 78° 39.861'W	Difficulty: moderate
GPS, vista: 39° 41.894'N, 78° 40.401'W	Distance: 1.5 miles
Faces: 024°	Time: 1 hour
Field of view: 316° to 92°	Elevation change: 260 feet
Relief: 60 feet	Best lenses: 20mm to 200mm
Elevation difference: 166 feet	Directions: See page 144.

This view is lost to history and doesn't appear on the park map. I assume it was a popular tourist attraction many decades ago due to the old carriage road network crisscrossing the hill you'll climb.

Walk around the yellow gate and down the gravel Old Hancock Road, passing a yellow and white post at .1 miles. At .23 miles pass a lone pine on the right with a large white vertical stripe on it. There may be a white U-turn arrow spray painted on the gravel road surface. At .35 miles (GPS coordinates: 39° 41.631'N, 78° 40.196W) look for an old woods road to the right; roadside brush will obscure it, so look several yards into the woods for a straight depression with parallel troughs and minimal undergrowth. Turn right to enter the woods and the road becomes obvious as a wide path with trampled leaf litter.

The path descends slightly, making a slow S to the left, then back to the right before straightening out. At .45 miles (GPS coordinates: 39° 41.672'N, 78° 40.296W) come to a Y which is the first of three rapid-fire, confusing intersections. Bear right and go about 70 paces to where you're presented with a blowdown where a tree trunk has been bent into an arch-like

Rocky Gap. Fall color was pretty good here, but nothing I had shot really spoke to me until I decided to shoot a self portrait. Even with a 25-second delay it took some real hustle to get in place. After fifteen tries, I was a bit winded. *Canon EOS 5D Mkii, Canon 20-105L, polarizer, ISO100 setting, f8 @ 1/30s*

shape. Go around, being careful to pick up the trail a couple paces beyond the arch.

You're now at a T intersection with a wide woods road. Twenty feet to your left is another T intersection where you can see a road coming downhill. To the right is a large blowdown blocking the road. Go the 20 feet to your left, then go right onto the sunken road that comes downhill toward you. Walk straight uphill a total of 26 paces, come to a Y (GPS coordinates: 39° 41.690′N, 78° 40.343W) and go right. You're now going steeply uphill along a meandering and heavily trod footpath, arriving at the view at .75 miles.

The view consists of two easily accessible triangular sandstone slabs that tilt upward at the end. The lower slab, which is the largest, is simple to walk

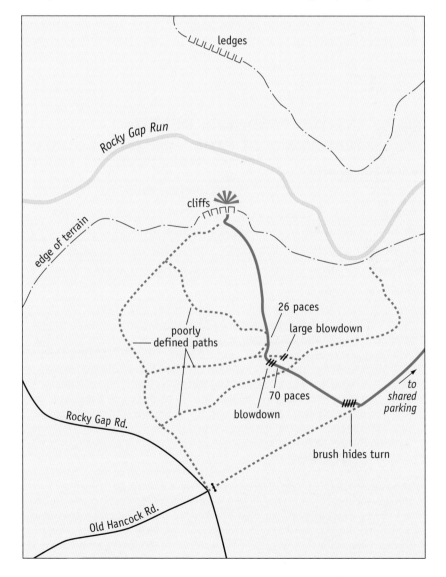

out onto. The upper one is a free-standing pillar that requires you to cross a 2-feet-wide gap over a 30-feet-deep fissure. It's one simple step, but probably not for someone uncomfortable around unprotected cliffs.

Set-ups are simple and I recommend a low tripod setting where you can sit comfortably behind the camera. The ridge opposite is Evitts Mountain and you'll note some exposed ledges below the summit, one of them quite large. Don't bother with them, as the approach from above is somewhat unnerving.

On your return, take great care with the rapid fire turns. It's easy to get turned around and end up either deep in Rocky Gap Run below Canyon Overlook or popping out along Rocky Gap Road about a half mile west.

If you have time, you can certainly climb Evitts Mountain and explore the Evitts home site or go all the way to a pipeline "vista" at the Mason-Dixon Line. If you want to do some graphic shooting, there are some awesome rock exposures below the dam on the white trail. Also, the aviary can be a lot of fun.

Hike 57 Warrior Mountain Wildlife Management Area, Allegany County

Spanish Leather Road

Type: ridge	**Relief:** 5 feet
Rating: 4	**Elevation difference:** 610 feet
GPS, parking: 39° 37.475′N, 78° 36.444′W	**Height:** 1,595 feet
GPS, vista: 39° 37.475′N, 78° 36.444′W	**Best time:** sunrise to early morning
Faces: 50°	**Best lenses:** 50mm to 400mm
Field of view: 30° to 70°	

Directions: From I-68 exit 56 at Flintstone, cross MD-144, pass between a general store and a diner to follow Murley's Branch Road southwest away from the interstate for 3.7 miles, and join Williams Road. In 1.9 miles bear left at a Y onto the poorly signed Cresap Mill Road, then make the left onto Oliver Beltz Road. (It'll look like a farm lane.) If you miss the Y, just keep going and make the left onto Oliver Beltz Road in about 1.0 miles. Oliver Beltz Road will switch back several times, and in 3.8 miles make a right onto Spanish Leather Road. A house sits next to the turn and Spanish Leather Road looks like a coarse gravel driveway or farm lane. Head about .3 miles up the road and park on the right where you feel comfortable. The tree line ahead hides a WMA parking lot, but it's okay to park roadside. GPS coordinates: 39° 37.475′N, 78° 36.444′W.

Note: Spanish Leather Road has fist-sized gravel and it can be tough going in a small car, so take your time. After several days of rain I did have to use 4WD to get through the first 30 yards. If you have a car-mounted GPS, it may try to bring you in from the west over Rocky Road Lane—do not do this. Beyond the WMA parking area, Rocky Road Lane and Spanish Leather Road are 4WD, high clearance only and Rocky Road Lane is heavily signed as private even though it's a township road.

Warrior Mountain. Standing on the roof of my car with a 400mm lens on a tripod required some degree of stealth. Shifting my weight, coughing, or even crossing my arms would cause the image to smear. Mirror lock-up is vital in these situations. *Canon EOS 5D Mkii, Tamron 200-400, polarizer, ISO400 setting, f16 @ 1/6s*

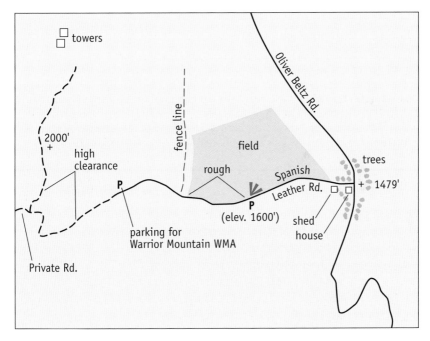

Once your vehicle's parking brake is set, hop on the roof and shoot away. The view is very subtle but when there's fog in the valley it's a great spot to go long and have hills and ridges peeking through. The view is in the general direction of Troutman Road (Hike 54). The field ahead of you will be golden yellow in fall and the mountains beyond will be awash in muted color. On my first trip in daylight I had a heck of a time finding this spot, as several road signs were missing and two didn't match my Gazetteer. On the way out after a fall sunrise shoot, I decided to explore the narrow back roads. Although I got thoroughly lost, I encountered several painters along Bear Hill Road to the east and we shared some notes. Now, these were locals and none of them seemed to be able to tell me where I was or how to get back to Flintstone. Two of them had a bit of debate over my map and each dropped a finger where they thought they were. I finally fired up my E-Trex and marked the location on the map. Simultaneously, they said, "Well, that isn't right." It was a lovely morning and I still had coffee in my mug, so I explored some more. You see I never get lost—I scout for locations and explore.

Hike 58 Finzel Swamp Preserve, Garrett County

Best times: Early spring and fall, any time of day	**Elev. Change:** 50 feet
Trail: 1.3 miles	**Gear:** 17mm to 200mm plus macro
Time: 45 minutes	

Directions: From I-68 exit 29, take MD-546/Beall School Road north toward the village of Finzel. In 1.8 miles turn right onto Cranberry Swamp Road (there will be a ball field on the right); if you pass a red barn on the left, you went 50 yards too far. In .1 miles bear left at a fork that will look like you're on somebody's driveway, but that's okay. Park at the road's end in a large gravel lot, bearing right as you enter to park on the lot's swamp-facing side. GPS coordinates: 39° 41.995'N, 78° 56.773'W.

This little gem is owned by The Nature Conservancy and you can read more about it at http://www.nature.org/ourinitiatives/regions/north america/unitedstates/maryland_dc/placesweprotect/finzel-swamp.xml. Finzel Swamp is listed by Audubon as an important birding area (IBA) and also by the Maryland Native Plant Society as a must-see. I agree with all of them—no matter what your calling is, Finzel Swamp is an ice-age gem waiting for you to explore it.

As you face a small pond fronting the lot, head right to a wide path cut through the brush. This old road, or perhaps a water control dike, runs straight across the swamp. A nice view opens up at the second bridge. From here, you get a look at a large tower that sits atop Sampson Rock (which is on private land and has no view). Another good shooting spot is at a culvert just beyond. Every direction you look in offers another interesting plant, tree, or shrub. Take your time—there's no hurry.

You'll arrive at a fence with some Nature Conservancy signage at .26 miles. To the left is a short path to what appears to be an old storage shed for

Finzel Swamp Preserve. I had hoped to get some really serious star trails, but the thin veil of clouds and sky glow eliminated that possibility. Instead, I settled on shorter exposures to manage the sky glow. A new moon would have also helped. *Canon EOS 5D Mkii, Canon 20-105L, ISO1800 setting, f8 @ 12:31s*

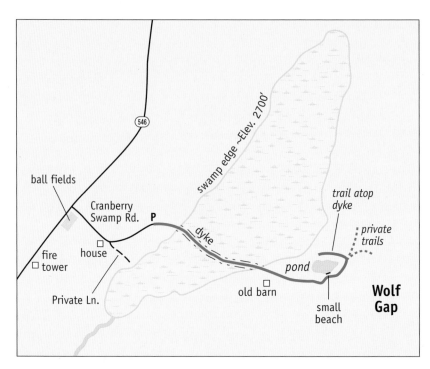

Finzel Swamp Preserve. The old farm pond and swamp was like glass in the early dawn, so mirror images it was. I must have shot hundreds of different compositions, all before the sun came up. *Canon EOS 5D Mkii, Canon 20-105L, ISO100 setting, f8 @ 3.2s*

the farm that once stood here. Continue along and find an old barn foundation at .41 miles. Here you can shoot patterns in the stone. At .45 miles come
to a T; to the right is an ATV trail that goes up a hill. The trail goes a little way
before ending at a blue post marking the end of the conservancy property.
Left takes you to one of the best spots here—the old farm pond. Go left.

In a few yards, arrive at a handsome pond. A little farther on, the trail
leaves the dike by dropping right, away from the pond. This is the end of the
road, and the conservancy property ends here. If you look carefully, you'll
note that one woods road continues in a northerly direction as another
climbs a hill toward the east. What you can't see (unless you look very
hard), are some posts, hidden among rhododendrons, with pale blue paint
on them—the universal sign of a private land boundary. Sorry, but everything beyond the pond is out of bounds.

An overgrown path circumnavigates the pond. From the south side near a
little beach-let, you can shoot panoramics of the surrounding forest. From
the east side you can get a good shot of the flanking western hill that defines
that side of the swamp's bowl. The grass is tall, and in the summer ticks will
be an issue; however, in the fall when the nights get frosty the ticks are gone
and you can wander through fields with abandon. I was so taken with this
little lost chunk of Canada that is the head of the Savage River that I
returned six times. I shot at dawn and midday, and photographed star trails
at night. This is one of my favorite places in this guide; no one is around to
bother you, and the critters don't seem to care that you're here.

Hike 59 Meadow Mountain Tower, Garrett County

Type: ledge	Height: 2,932 feet
Rating: 5	Best time: sunrise, full moon
GPS, parking: 39° 34.760′N, 79° 12.050′W	Difficulty: moderate
GPS, vista: 39° 34.209′N, 79° 12.512′W	Distance: 1.7 miles
Faces: 145°	Time: 50 minutes
Field of view: 100° to 190°	Elevation change: 180 feet
Relief: 20 feet	Best lenses: 35mm to 400mm
Elevation difference: 980 feet	

Directions: From the entrance to New Germany State Park, take New Germany
Road south for 5.7 miles and make a hard right on Brenneman Road. Brenneman
Road meets New Germany at a very acute angle and trees block the turn. (If you
miss it, you'll come to Monroe Run Vista [Hike 60]. Make a U-turn and backtrack
.4 miles.) Brenneman Road climbs steeply, and in .4 miles you'll come to a wide
area marked by two signs and a large yellow gate. Park on the right, but don't
block the gate. GPS coordinates: 39° 34.760′N, 79° 12.050′W.

ross the road heading southwest on a wide, well-graded, off-road vehicle (ORV) trail and climb steadily but agreeably for .3 miles, then drop
before climbing again. At .8 miles come to a view cutout on the left. The
trail is rocky during the climb but grassy after that. The tower is long since
gone and the foundation remnants impossible to find. The best shooting
perch is a small ledge about 5 feet down from the plateau atop the ridge.

At the view's extreme right is a power line cut, which is easy to keep out
of frame. On the left, at 164°, is a fine-looking cabin. What's most troubling
is the extent of gypsy moth damage and deforestation. A large stand of
denuded white snags dominates the left, with one lone tree at the extreme
left. Ridges throughout the view are dotted with dead trees in large and
small numbers. When I shot this in the fall the snags were less of an issue,
and obviously in snow cover it won't matter a bit.

Meadow Mountain. This is by far my favorite image in this guide. This is why I lace up my
boots at 4 A.M.—locations like this and days like these are rare and should be savored.
Canon EOS 5D Mkii, Canon 20-105L, 2 stop graduate, ISO100 setting, f8 @ .8s

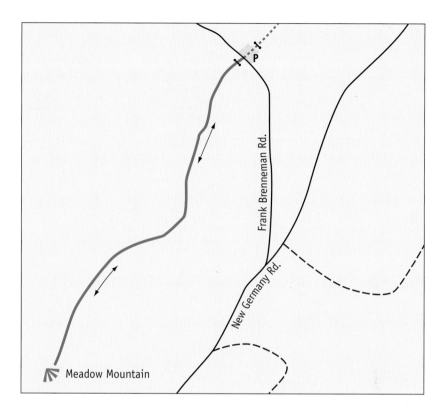

Meadow Mountain

Hike 60 Monroe Run Vista, Savage River State Forest, Garrett County

Type: ridge	**Height:** 2,475 feet
Rating: 4	**Best time:** late morning to early afternoon and full moon
GPS, parking: 39° 34.049'N, 79° 12.298'W	**Difficulty:** easy
GPS, vista: 39° 34.049'N, 79° 12.298'W	**Distance:** 50 yards
Faces: 130°	**Time:** 10 minutes
Field of view: 110° to 150°	**Elevation change:** 20 feet
Relief: 20 feet	**Best lenses:** 50mm to 250mm
Elevation difference: 510 feet	

Directions: From the entrance to New Germany State Park, follow New Germany Road south for 6.2 miles to a parking area and picnic pavilion on the left just after passing Brennaman Road on the right. A chainsaw sculpture of an eagle sits next to the parking area. GPS coordinates: 39° 34.049'N, 79° 12.298'W

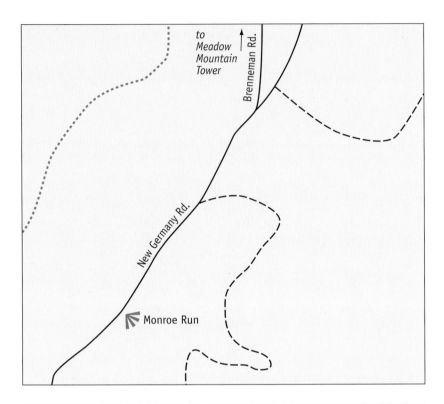

Monroe Run Vista. Looks like a midday image, doesn't it? Well, it's shot by the full moon around midnight. I had to shoot several frames with noise reduction off to properly place the graduated filter, kind of like night vision assistance. Once I was set, I reset the noise filter to maximum and shot about a dozen frames, taking over an hour. Camera processing time was actually longer than the exposure, totaling nearly eight minutes per frame. *Canon EOS 5D Mkii, Canon 20-105L, 1 stop graduate, ISO1600 setting, f8 @ 2:30*

alk down a little path to a stone wall at the view and set up to the wall's left. There are several trees framing the view; if they impinge on your shot just walk around the wall. The view is kept pretty tidy. Use a medium to long lens to isolate the nested ridges. Looking down on Monroe Run (which can't be seen), the valley cuts from left to right, opening a nice graphic image that is best in fall color. The two ridges don't have names, but the left side divides out Whiskey Hollow and the right divides out Bushwhack Run. Out of view along the view axis is Big Run State Park. I enjoyed shooting graphic landscapes lit by the full moon. It made for a very late night, but the images had a soft, surreal texture. It was quite fun.

Hike 61 State Land High Point, Garrett County

Type: ledge	**Height:** 3,020 feet
Rating: 3	**Best time:** late afternoon through sunset and moonlight
GPS, parking: 39° 27.772'N, 79° 11.475'W	**Difficulty:** moderate
GPS, vista: 39° 27.929'N, 79° 11.562'W	**Distance:** .5 miles
Faces: 320°	**Time:** 30 minutes
Field of view: 300° to 008°	**Elevation change:** 111 feet
Relief: 12 feet	**Best lenses:** 20mm to 200mm
Elevation difference: 1,102 feet	

Directions: From the entrance of New Germany State Park, take New Germany Road south for 7.8 miles and bear left to join MD-495 south. Follow MD-495 south for 7.4 miles and make a left at a T onto Swanton Road (a house on the left has a footbridge over a creek in front of it). Take Swanton Road for 2.1 miles and turn left onto MD-135. In .5 miles park on the right in a wide gravel area near two telephone poles, just north of Walnut Bottom Road. GPS coordinates: 39° 27.772'N, 79° 11.475'W.

camper across the road to a gravel pathway and climb steeply through a pine forest for .22 miles. When you get to some rhododendrons and boulders, follow the most well-worn path to exposed sandstone ledges at .25 miles. The view is slowly becoming overgrown by black birch; however, it's so well known among the locals that a group comes in every few years and cleans it up.

Walk along the ledges and explore several setups. The best position is well to the left of where the field of view is more northerly. From here, trees surrounding the view are not an issue and the sandstone surface has an interesting texture for use as a foreground. The large towers in the distance along an axis of 330° are the ones above Deep Creek Lake. If you go to the extreme right, the westerly view opens but trees will be an issue in the middle

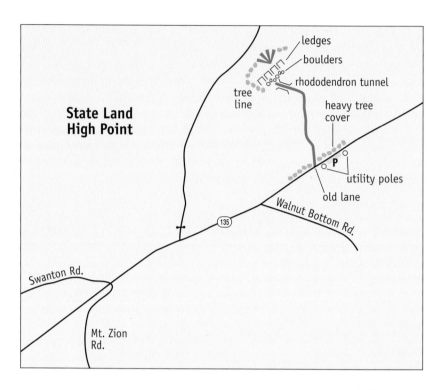

State Land High Point

ledges

boulders

rhododendron tunnel

tree line

heavy tree cover

utility poles

P

old lane

Walnut Bottom Rd.

135

Swanton Rd.

Mt. Zion Rd.

State Land High Point. Sunset was a washed-out bust, with no color and lots of contrails. When faced with this, wait until well after sunset and shoot the landscape lit by the pastels of twilight. Note how the rocks on the left of this pan sequence pick up the color of the sky. There was enough light to get the trees to continue to glow, even twenty minutes after the sun went down. *Canon EOS 5D Mkii, Canon 20-105L, 2 stop graduate, ISO400 setting, f8 @ 1/6*

distance. Fall is the best time, since all the surrounding trees will be a mono-chrome green the rest of the year. It's also a quick snowshoe to get here in fresh snow. I came here several times when I was shooting this book and found that the best shooting is in twilight, after the sun goes down. Earth shadow was very distinct in autumn.

At this point, you might ask why I don't have a hike to the true Maryland high point, the 3,360-foot Hoye-Crest on Backbone Mountain in the extreme southwest corner of Garrett County. Good question. This is a guide for hik-ers and photographers, and Hoye-Crest doesn't have a view. It's a large stone cairn sitting upon an unimpressive hump in the woods with a large sil-ver sign next to it. Although on private land, Hoye-Crest is open to the pub-lic and easily accessed from US-219 in West Virginia in Monongahela National Forest. Go there if you'd like, but don't bother lugging anything other than a cell phone to take pictures.

Hike 62 High Rock Tower, Garrett County

Type: ledge	**Height:** 2,991 feet
Rating: 5+	**Best time:** late afternoon through sunset and late night
GPS, parking: 39° 32.603'N, 79° 4.797'W	**Difficulty:** difficult
GPS, vista: 39° 32.672'N, 79° 5.808'W	**Distance:** 2.2 miles
Faces: 300°	**Time:** 1 hour
Field of view: 220° to 020° from ledges; 360° circle from tower	**Elevation change:** 570 feet
Relief: 20 feet	**Best lenses:** 17mm to 100mm
Elevation difference: 1,510 feet	

Directions: From the entrance of New Germany State Park, take McAndrews Hill Road past the campground and follow it for 1.4 miles, then turn right at a T onto Westernport Road. In 7.9 miles park at wide spot on the left near a yellow gate. A woods road descends steeply left and a gravel road climbs steeply across the road right. GPS coordinates: 39° 32.603'N, 79° 4.797'W.

Westernport Road is a major commuter route and traffic tends to fly downhill, so run carefully across the road. Begin the steep ascent up the gravel road to the tower site. The overgrown gravel road is relentless with a constant 10 percent grade; however, the payoff is huge. When you get to the tower, pass it on the left and follow a well-worn path through sticker bushes to the west-facing ledges atop Big Savage Mountain.

To the south, you can see the wind turbines along the summit ridge of Eagle Rock 14 miles away, while to the north the view is limitless. With the

old building foundation behind you and to your left, look for the one ledge boulder that's sculpted like a lounge chair and have a well-deserved seat. The trees surrounding the view area are just tall enough to make any west-facing shot require a longer lens. Shots facing north can be wider, using the exposed rocks as anchoring foregrounds. If you can tolerate

High Rock Tower. I shot the cliffs and ledges at sunset and then climbed up to the third platform just to see what there was to see. That's when I noticed the side-lit glow of the trees. Shot about ten minutes after sunset, the trees continued to glow for the next half hour. Just magical. *Canon EOS 5D Mkii, Canon 20-105L, 1 stop graduate, ISO400 setting, f8 @ 1/6*

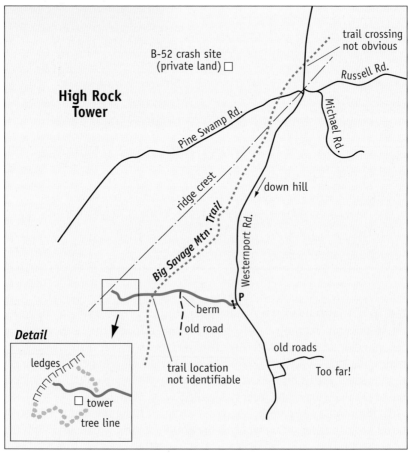

State Land High Point. The rising moon is a little higher than I would like, but the glow of the trees and the distinctive Earth shadow work well together. The pale blue line, with the pink glow above, is the Earth's own shadow in the atmosphere and getting it takes some planning and very clear weather. *Canon EOS 5D Mkii, Canon 20-105L, 1 stop graduate, ISO400 setting, f8 @ .6*

the chilly breezes of night, this is the best spot in the area to shoot star trails.

Now head back to the tower and climb no farther than the third landing, holding the handrails and testing the stairs as you go. (The stairs are in good shape but it's still a good idea to play it safe.) There's no need to climb farther, since to the southwest there are houses along Pine Swamp Road, including a very handsome one atop Rhodes Hill, that come into view. The view to the east suffers from a similar issue—this is why low is better than high. Also, the tower cab is home to numerous vultures and it's best to just leave them be. When you've soaked up the fine view, head down the steep road to your car, arriving at 2.2 miles. (Don't forget to carefully sprint across the road.)

Once back at your car, there's one other thing to do if you have the time. As you head back up Westernport Road, turn right onto Swamp Road at the summit and drive north about 1.0 miles to the first wind turbine you see. You can park nearby. If you shoot a wide angle late at night with a fraction of the moon illuminated, you can create a surreal image of the smeared blade disk with star trails in the background. I never had the time to do this, but I've seen some amazing images done by others.

If you purchased a Savage River State Forest map, you may have noted a small triangle marking the location of the 1962 B-52 crash site along the Big Savage Mountain trail on the northeast side of Westernport Road. That is wrong. The crash site is on private land on the southwest side of Westernport. (The crash actually happened on January 13, 1964.) There were two 9-megaton yield Mark-53 thermonuclear weapons being ferried when the plane's tail was torn off in winter storm. Unfortunately, you can't access the site, which is a shame.

Hike 63 Potomac Overlook and Cascade Falls, Garrett County

Potomac Overlook

Type: cliff	**Height:** 1,909 feet
Rating: 3	**Best time:** early morning or damp overcast
GPS, parking: 39° 21.741'N, 79° 14.108'W	**Difficulty:** easy
GPS, vista: 39° 21.879'N, 79° 13.995'W	**Distance:** .3 miles
Faces: 218°	**Time:** 30 minutes
Field of view: 210° to 230°	**Elevation change:** 80 feet
Relief: 70 feet	**Best lenses:** 20mm to 300mm
Elevation difference: 70 feet	

Cascade Falls

Type: slide over slide	**Difficulty:** easy
Rating: 4	**Distance:** .150 yards
GPS: 39° 21.938'N, 79° 14.710'W	**Time:** 20 minutes
Stream: Lostland Run	**Elevation change:** 50 feet
Height: 40 feet	**Best lenses:** 20mm to 70mm

Directions: Begin your short adventure to this nice view and fall from the town of Oakland at the intersection of 3rd Street and East Oak Street (US-219). Take US-219 southbound for .5 miles, bear left off of US-219 (which makes a right), and follow MD-135 south for 1.4 miles. As you make a long, sweeping left, pass the post office on your left and immediately turn right onto Paul Street. Go left in a couple blocks onto East 3rd Avenue (MD-560) as you pass a gas station on your right. Follow MD-560 for 1.9 miles and go left on Bethlehem Road. Take Bethlehem Road for 2.1 miles to a Y with Eagle Rock Road and go right to stay with Bethlehem Road. In 1.4 miles turn left onto Combination Road, then in .6 miles go left again on Potomac Camp Road. Turn right onto Lostland Run Road in .9 miles (after passing the forest office on your left). Drive 3.0 miles to the road's end and park. (You passed the parking area for Cascade Falls at 2.2 miles.) GPS coordinates: 39° 21.794'N, 79° 13.948'W.

Walk around the wooden barrier and follow a wide dirt path. In about 30 yards, bear left at a Y for Potomac Overlook. Just before you start a steepish climb up an ancient woods road, you'll pass massive stone slabs in the river on the right. Arrive at the walled view at .1 miles. Perched atop a 70-foot cliff, you'll find the view from here is restricted because of surrounding trees, so get low. It's an excellent fall color spot. About 50 feet before this walled area is an unmarked, better view made from some old timbers and poles. Sit down on these and you'll be able to get low enough to shoot under the surrounding trees.

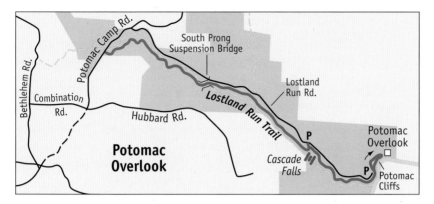

Damp conditions and/or high flow are a must to shoot from here since the river is filled with large white boulders. On a sunny day, the contrast will overwhelm your camera unless you plan on bracketing for a High Dynamic Range (HDR) image. From either view there is one small tree limb that will sneak into your frame's upper left, no matter how you compose the shot. This one of those times where I think Photoshop is perfectly okay.

If you'd like to continue following the river, please do. At .37 miles exit the state forest lands at an "abandoned camp" or party spot. Now at river level, you can rock hop into the river to almost halfway and shoot upstream.

Work back toward your car, and when you get back to the Y go left on the Cliffs Trail and head for the river's edge. End up exactly below the two high overlooks. Here you can explore the riffles and eddies along the bank and work the Potomac at river level. Use extreme caution climbing the rocks and moving along the bank—there are some deep holes and the current is swift, even in July. In damp weather, any boulder tilted toward the river is an invitation to disaster.

When you're done chasing images, head back to your car, arriving at .3 miles.

Move your car .8 miles up the road and park on the left in a large parking area signed "State Forest Parking, No Vehicles After 10PM." GPS coordinates: 39° 21.993′N, 79° 14.708′W.

Head downhill toward Lostland Run along a heavily used trail. In about 130 yards you'll come to stairs leading to the creek, while a white-blazed trail goes left. Head down the stairs (one section is closed so a little scramble is required). Cascade Falls is made of two slides separated by a dozen yards. Each drop is nice and can be shot individually, but combined they are quite wonderful. Below the lower drop are extensive cobble bars from which you can work. To get to these cobbles, work downstream on the run's left-hand side (the side you're on) and look for a couple large rocks jutting into the run. You can rock hop from here. Set your camera as high as you can so you show the separation between the drops.

I strongly encourage you to explore this delightfully quiet run upstream from the falls. If you get back to where you found the white-blazed trail, go

Cove Mountain Overlook. As a nature shooter I've never been fond of "industrial" roadside pullout views. I like stuff that you have get a little sweaty for. However, this is a perfect exception. Standing on my Jeep's roof during midday, this isn't bad for fifteen minutes of work, is it? *Canon EOS 5D Mkii, Canon 20-105L, 2 stop graduate, ISO100 setting, f8 @ 1/40*

left and head upstream a short distance to just above the cascade's head. When the white-blazed trail goes right and uphill, go left on an old footpath that hugs the creek edge. Hop in at any point it's convenient and just shoot away. Go wide to shoot woodland scenes or go longer to explore the myriad of graphic designs found wherever water tumbles over and around rock. I followed the white-blazed trail well upstream and found that the shooting petered out about 50 yards above the falls. Take your time and enjoy a delightful damp day in Lostland Run.

Hike 64 US-219 Vista, Garrett County

Cove Run

Type: ridge	**Height:** 2,767 feet
Rating: 4	**Best time:** late afternoon through sunset
GPS, parking: 39° 40.756′N, 79° 17.244′W	**Difficulty:** easy
GPS, vista: 39° 40.756′N, 79° 17.244′W	**Distance:** 50 yards
Faces: 267°	**Time:** 10 minutes
Field of view: 210° to 325°	**Elevation change:** none
Relief: 20 feet	**Best lenses:** 20mm to 300mm
Elevation difference: 594 feet	

Directions: From I-68 exit 14 for Keysers Ridge, take US-219 south for 2.1 miles. Turn right at a small blue sign for the viewpoint and park in the large parking area.

Head to the fence and hop up on the guardrail to get your lens above the fence. I shot from the roof of my Jeep. The view cutout leaves a scraggly foreground; however, the trees downslope are healthy and make a pleasant foreground when shooting with a medium lens. A farm on the view's left side is mirrored by one on the right. The one on the left is red with one silo, and the one to the right is white with four silos. Pale roofing on the right farm will be an issue around the noon hour but this can be "fixed" with either careful framing or by using the "fix" tool in Photoshop. Along 310° there's a cell tower but it doesn't impact the scene too badly. Facing west to northwest, you'll be able to shoot summer sunsets as panoramics and stitch them together. Several picnic tables make this a nice spot to relax between the several western Garrett County hikes. Enjoy!

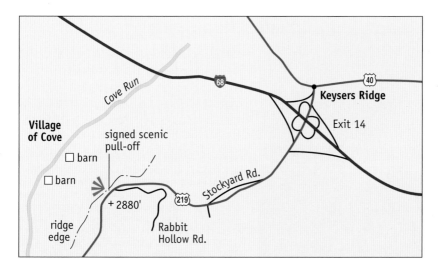

Hike 65 Cranesville Swamp, Garrett County, Maryland, and Preston County, West Virginia

Type: walk	**Distance:** 1.3 miles
Rating: 5	**Time:** 1 hour
GPS: 39° 31.907'N, 79° 29.128'W	**Elevation change:** 60 feet
Best time: sunrise through midmorning, late afternoon	**Best lenses:** 17mm to 100mm, plus macro
Difficulty: easy	

Directions: Cranesville Swamp is a little off the beaten path and it's easy to miss the last turn. From I-68 Exit 4 at Friendsville, take MD-42/Friendsville Road west (I-68 will be on your left) for 1.4 miles. Turn left onto Blooming Rose Road at the cemetery and immediately cross I-68. Take Blooming Rose Road for 1.2 miles and make a hard right to keep with Blooming Rose Road. In another 1.8 miles turn left onto White Rock Road. (If you miss this, you'll cross into West Virginia when the road becomes CR-11.) Follow the narrow White Rock Road for 4.2 miles, pass an open field on the left, and go right onto Cranesville Swamp Road. There will be a small house on the left corner opposite the turn. In 5.1 miles turn right onto Lake Ford Road. In .1 miles cross into West Virginia and the road changes names to Burnside Camp/CR-49. In another .2 miles bear right onto the gravel Feather Lane and head up the narrow lane. Turn right near a set of power lines at a tiny little sign for Cranesville Swamp Preserve and park here. GPS coordinates: 39° 31.907' N 79° 29.128' W.

Cranesville Swamp is a Nature Conservancy property and it's a wonderful bit of the arctic lost in a bowl-shaped valley on the Maryland–West Virginia line. The property is open year round from dawn to dusk. There's 5.5 miles of trail, but you're interested in just 1.3 miles of them, particularly the boardwalk section that traverses the swamp itself.

From the smallish parking area follow the blue-blazed trail. In about 500 feet the

Cranesville Swamp. Curses, foiled again! That's the only way to explain my bad luck at such a wonderful spot. An attempted early fall shot was spoiled by Irene, by then a big snowstorm that dumped over a foot of snow. With the next season came Sandy and a couple feet of snow. So this is it, a handheld midsummer shot. Frustration doesn't begin to describe it. *Canon EOS 5D Mkii, Canon 20-105L, 1 stop graduate, ISO100 setting, f8 @ 1/50*

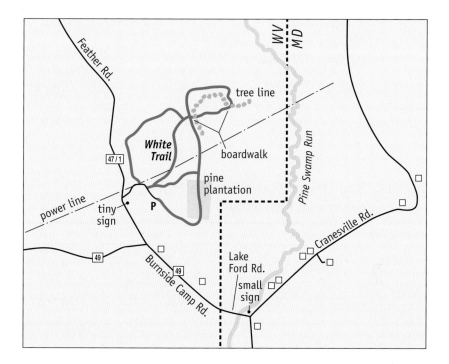

tight, twisty trail breaks into a pine plantation, which would make for some nice shooting in fog when it blankets the swamp in cooler weather. Keep an eye out for plump blueberries in late June and early July—they're delightfully sweet! The trail makes a couple more jogs then straightens out, and at .29 miles the yellow-blazed trail joins from the left. Just beyond, cross under a power line with expanses of marsh grass on the right.

Come to an intersection with the orange-blazed loop trail at .43 miles. To the right begins the boardwalk, ahead is your return route, and to the left is the orange-blazed trail. Go right and move slowly out into the swamp. The next 100 yards are magic and if you bring macro gear here in the spring it will take at least an hour to move that 100 yards. Morning mist is best, although evening is nice as well. However, in early morning everything will be dew covered and dragonflies will be perched and motionless, covered in it. Take your time—the swamp has been here since the last ice age ended and it'll be here tomorrow.

The boardwalk ends at .61 miles at the tree line, and the soil texture and character changes just a few paces from it. Keep a sharp eye out for garter snakes and frogs, which live here in large numbers. I saw several deer— really big deer—and I would assume that come November they know where to hunker down.

Rejoin the blue- and orange-blazed trail at .79 miles. It's hiker's choice for the return. The blue-blazed trail is the straight shot return and I prefer it since the other trails through the forest don't have much going on photographically.

When you get back to the pine plantation stop for a different perspective, then speed hike back to the car, arriving at 1.3 miles.

I was a little unlucky during my two trips. I couldn't get here until early July so the plants were well past peak, plus it had been hot and dry for a couple weeks so nothing looked particularly perky. Cranesville is on my list of places to return to in prime season; I'm just sorry it won't be in time to get the images off to the publisher.

Hike 66 Swallow Falls State Park, Garrett County

Muddy Falls

Type: fall	Stream: Muddy Run
Rating: 5	Height: 60 feet
GPS: 39° 30.067'N, 79° 25.084'W	

Lower Falls

Type: fall	GPS: 39° 29.956'N, 79° 24.932'W
Rating: 1	Height: 8 feet

Swallow Falls

Type: slide	Stream: Youghiogheny River
Rating: 4	Height: 22 feet
GPS: 39° 29.750'N, 79° 25.050'W	

Tolliver Falls

Type: fall	Stream: Tolliver Creek
Rating: 3	Height: 6 feet
GPS: 39° 29.688'N, 79° 25.106'W	
Difficulty: easy	Elevation change: 170 feet
Distance: 1.25 miles	Best lenses: 20mm to 70mm
Time: 1 hour	

Directions: From I-68 Interchange 14, take US-219 South for 12.1 miles, passing US-219 View (Hike 64) and crossing Deep Creek Lake. Go left onto Mayhew Inn Road. Mayhew Inn Road is quite curvy, and as it follows Deep Creek Lake there will be a number of businesses with tourists not paying much attention to what's coming at them, so be aware of other inattentive drivers. Follow Mayhew Inn Road for 4.3 miles and bear left onto Oakland Sang Run Road, then in .3 miles go right onto Swallow Falls Road for 1.3 miles. As soon as you cross the Youghiogheny River, go right onto Maple Glade Road, cross Tolliver Creek, and park on the right at the visitor center. GPS coordinates: 39° 29.948'N, 79° 25.130'W.

From the large parking area, head under the arch announcing the Canyon Trail and at the T go left for Muddy Creek Falls. When you get to the handicapped parking area, bear right onto a boardwalk that will take you several paces to the falls overlook. The creek cuts across a sandstone layer on the far side. This cap rock is a relatively horizontal layer within the complexly cross-bedded Pottsville Group. The wide expanse of pale stone before you is contrasted by the nearly black formation of the fall and the deep green of hemlock and rhododendrons on the far side. It'll be impossible to shoot unless the cap rock is wet.

Exit the platform and move down the stairs to the fall's base. There is one decent spot along the stairs; however, foreground trees and sneakers will be an issue, along with crowding. There are a number of excellent spots from the easily accessible creek looking upstream. A bridge above the fall's head provides access to both banks, so take time to work Muddy Run well upstream of the fall. The major issue is other people. The fall's head is easily accessible, so you'll have be super patient. Get here midweek or when it's wet.

Head downstream and quickly come to the confluence of Muddy Run with the much larger Youghiogheny River. Muddy Run begins as a quiet stream

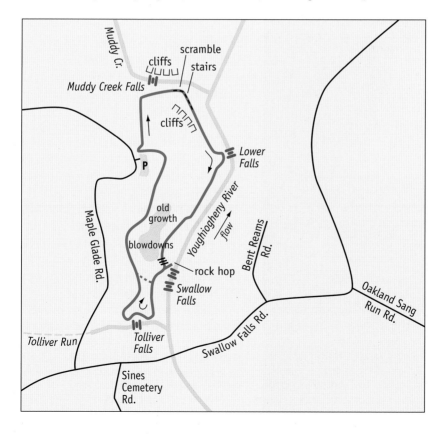

within Cranesville Swamp (Hike 65), whereas the Youghiogheny begins at Silver Lake 17 miles south-southwest, just across the border in West Virginia. The Youghiogheny comes from the right, overwhelms the flow of Muddy Run, then sweeps to the left as it curves quickly away. It's an easy scramble to the water's edge but take great care—the Youghiogheny runs swift and deep. From here, you can see the large elevation drop as the Youghiogheny heads north through the canyon; 8 miles away is Gap Falls, followed by a big rapid called National Falls, both of which are on private lands.

Continue along the trail, heading upstream with the Youghiogheny on your left, climb some stairs, and come to the long side. Cliffs now hover on the right as you continue to ascend parallel to this not-too-picturesque slide. As soon as the cliffs disappear, a side trail drops left to the slide's head. Looking downstream, you'll see that the ledge you were perched on at the confluence was radically undercut and is supported by three thin pillars. Just food for thought.

Back on the rocky main trail, a very short distance brings you to the 8-foot ledge of Lower Falls. Side trails abound and you can easily get to the head or tailwater. Visible upstream is Swallow Falls; you can easily frame both, but the large expanses of tan rock will need to be wet for the image to

render properly. Plus, Sallow's head is completely open, so in overcast weather the fall's head will just be a bunch of blank white blinkies. If you've earned some good karma, you'll get lucky and have partly cloudy skies and a wet foreground that's in shade. Halfway between the two falls, a large old-growth hemlock blowdown cuts across the trail. Hang a left and follow an obvious path down to the water's edge; from here you'll be able to work Swallow Falls by itself.

Swallow Falls is a steep slide that cuts from right to left and has a dead pine jutting from it, so keep that out of frame. It's easy rock hopping to get to a comfortable rock slab well into the river where you can center-frame the fall.

The hemlock grove ("Sensitive Management Area" on the map) is a very special

Muddy Creek Falls. Good cloud cover, no people, and you have a photograph. Shot at 20mm using a hyperfocal technique with my lens about 20 inches from the water. *Canon EOS 5D Mkii, Canon 20-105L, polarizer, ISO100 setting, f22 @ .6*

Tolliver Falls. I waited for clouds to cover the scene to even out an unworkable contrast problem. The fall didn't work well as an isolated portrait, so I tilted up to show its place among a lovely hemlock grove. A long exposure filled the weakly flowing fall. *Canon EOS 5D Mkii, Canon 20-105L, polarizer, ISO100 setting, f22 @ 10s*

place—it's a 40-acre old-growth forest. Old growth anything is rare anywhere in the east. The best photography here is when there's fog or light rain. Snow would be very nice as well.

In about 100 yards above Swallow Falls, follow the trail hard left to enter the small Tolliver Creek. Tolliver Falls sits above a boulder choke, and it's a 6-foot ledge enveloped by hemlocks. Small though it may be, this was perhaps my favorite spot in the park. Muddy Falls is big and powerful, but Tolliver Falls is a subtle bit of nature's artwork. From here, the trail climbs away from the creek and runs parallel to the road to the parking area. I recommend keeping with the creek shed for a while before backtracking to the trail. Tolliver Creek has a lot of small burbles and pleasant graphic possibilities. Take your time here and enjoy—there's plenty of time to make the short walk to the parking lot.

About the Author

Scott Brown lives in Bristol, Pennsylvania, and is an engineering professional and high school teacher. He is also an avid hiker, trail runner, outdoor photographer, and author of *Pennsylvania Waterfalls*, *Pennsylvania Mountain Vistas*, and *New York Waterfalls*. His articles have been published in *Nature Photographer* and *Pennsylvania Magazine* and his photographs have appeared in *Blue Ridge Country*, *Country*, *Country Extra*, and the book *American Vision*.

The author at the summit of Mount Evans, Colorado—14,265 feet.